12/15

THE KANSAS CITY STAR.

Crowned

The story of the relentless Kansas City Royals and their brilliant run to a World Championship

JOHN SLEEZER

 KANSAS CITY STAR BOOKS

Crowned

The story of the relentless Kansas City Royals and their brilliant run to a World Championship

By the staff of The Kansas City Star.

Edited by Kent Richards
Book design by Bob Deck

Published by Kansas City Star Books
1729 Grand Blvd.
Kansas City, MO 64108

First edition
ISBN 978-1-61169-161-0

Printed in the United States of America
by Walsworth Publishing Co., Inc.,
Marceline, Mo.

Produced by Mission Point Press,
Traverse City, Mich.

www.TheKansasCityStore.com

www.kansascity.com

KANSAS CITY STAR BOOKS

Photograph, pages 2-3: *The Royals pose for a group shot after their World Series victory and locker-room celebration.*

Photograph, pages 4-5: *About 800,000 fans turned out for a parade and celebration honoring the team on the Tuesday following the final win.*

SHANE KEYSER

Table of Contents

JOHN SLEEZER

THIS IS THE TEAM THAT KANSAS CITIANS WILL BRAG ABOUT TO THEIR KIDS, TO THEIR GRANDKIDS, AND MAYBE EVEN THEIR KIDS' GRANDKIDS.

NEW YORK

The euphoria of a championship years in the making and once so fundamentally unrealistic filled an otherwise quiet stadium.

The only noise was from the men who earned this moment, and the fans who waited so long to feel it. The Royals are World Series champions. Is this real?

For years and years — decades, really — this was the kind of thing you could only see in your dreams, and even then, you'd wake up and realize how silly that was. The Royals, for so long the picture of failure, are baseball's champion. How did this happen?

The details will be memorized. Matt Harvey's dominance setting up one last wild comeback. Kelvin Herrera's three innings. Eric Hosmer's double and then his dash home in the ninth. Christian Colon's single, Alcides Escobar's double ... on and on it went in a five-run 12th until Wade Davis closed out one more win.

The Royals are World Series champions, finally and again. They beat the Mets 7-2 in Game 5. The best team in franchise history was honored with a parade along Grand Boulevard, the same route they took 30 years ago.

"Everything's just perfect, man," Hosmer said. "This is too good of a group, too good of a team, not to be remembered as world champions."

They won their championship the only way they should've won their championship, with another comeback in another late inning, a relentless group of friends and teammates who've known only success these last two years pushing a franchise that only knew failure for so long.

It was one last comeback for one of the greatest rally teams in 111 years of playoff baseball. The script is so well known by now that Dayton Moore, the general manager who envisioned this long before anyone else believed, turned to an assistant as his team went to bat at the start of the ninth inning, down by two, with nothing but belief in his heart.

"We're about ready to win a World Series," Moore said. "I can just feel it."

Every champion is remembered fondly, but this one is different even by that high standard. Some of that is in wiping away two decades of losing, and some of that is in the way they attacked every day, every game, every inning, every pitch. Kansas Citians bought more tickets than ever before this year, and spent more time watching on TV than ever before. Following this team became more than a pastime, and more than a habit. It is now an addiction.

This is the team that Kansas Citians will brag about to their kids, to their grandkids, and maybe even their kids' grandkids. This group has done more than win the world championship. That happens every year, for some lucky city. But not like this.

The Royals have rewritten not just a franchise's sorry history, but forever changed the way sports are viewed and loved and consumed in KC. Kansas City had not had a championship parade in 30 years, long enough that babies conceived and born in the years since have grown up to know sports success only as something that happens in other places. It is long enough that some of those kids are doctors, or war heroes. They have careers and mortgages and marriages. Some have divorced. This is a long time coming.

These Royals will be forever remembered for the forceful way they sliced through the regular season, and continually refusing to die in the playoffs. Eight of their 11 playoff wins came after trailing in the sixth inning or later. Six of those comebacks erased deficits of two runs or more. No other team has ever done that. You could live 100 more years and not see it again.

The eighth inning in Houston. Lorenzo Cain scoring the pennant-clinching run from first on a single, and Davis pitching both sides of a rain delay in Kansas City. The ball scooting past Daniel Murphy's glove and Hosmer's sprint home in New York. Baseball's playoffs create drama naturally, but the sport has never seen anything like this.

Others have won on budgets, but in modern baseball the Royals lifting the trophy with all those little flags on it is without precedent. The A's were celebrated with a best-selling book and a Brad Pitt movie, but Moneyball never played in the World Series. The Rays may be the closest cousin to what the Royals accomplished, but they lost their only World Series in five games. The Rockies built a pennant winner almost exclusively through their farm system, but were swept in their only World Series.

These Royals have shown baseball's hungriest market how to love the sport again, and that wishing for and even expecting good things to happen doesn't have to end in heartbreak.

Salvador Perez's relentlessness, Mike Moustakas' resiliency, Alex Gordon's determination, Cain's brilliance, Escobar's easiness, Davis' steadiness, Ned Yost's stubbornness and the patience of Glass and Moore — they are all irreplaceable parts of one of the great long-term turnarounds in professional sports history.

— *Sam Mellinger*

THE ROYALS SIMPLY WERE THE BEST TEAM IN BASEBALL AND HAVE A FINE CLAIM TO BEING ONE OF THE MOST COMPLETE AND INSPIRING IN RECENT YEARS.

A few hours before Game 5 of the 2015 World Series, Royals manager Ned Yost contemplated a question about whether he believed fate was an ally of his team.

This is the sort of question most in Yost's position, and Yost himself, typically would sneer at, mock and dismiss.

But this is what Yost said:

"Yeah, I do, I really do. I felt from the beginning that this group, after what they accomplished last year and (after seeing) the heartbreak in their eyes after Game 7, that had unfinished business to do.

"And, yeah, I sit there sometimes and think this is just the way it's supposed to be."

After pitcher Edinson Volquez's father died just before Game 1, making him a startling third Royal to lose a parent in just over two months, first baseman Eric Hosmer said, "It's just another angel above, just watching us and behind us through this whole run."

Then there was luck, which a small but vocal group of cynics suggested characterized the Royals — as if that somehow diminished their knack for manufacturing their own with their spirit and style of play and by alchemizing stray opportunities into gold.

All of these things forever will be associated with the 2015 Royals, whose World Series title ended a 30-year championship drought, purged decades of futility, validated a process launched by general manager Dayton Moore in 2006 and completed a quest propelled in earnest by the sting of losing Game 7 of the 2014 World Series.

None of these things, fate and angels and luck, were in any way considered part of the Royals' arsenal for most of the previous 29 years.

"If you didn't see it, you wouldn't believe it," misty-eyed Royals super-scout Art Stewart, who has been with the team since its inception in 1969, said after the Royals crushed the Mets 7-2 in 12 innings in Game 5 to put it away with an exclamation point after another signature comeback.

But maybe the part that's hardest to believe after so many excruciating years in between titles and even competency is that all of this is entirely explainable without any otherworldly suggestions whatsoever.

The Royals simply were the best team in baseball and have a fine claim to being one of the most complete and inspiring in recent years.

In fact, but for a prescribed September retooling that made for a rough month and limited them to a 95-win regular season even as it helped gird them for the long haul, they might be a nominee for being among the most notable in the history of the game.

If that sounds hyperbolic, consider the captivating relish with which they played; their remarkable defense and bullpen and reservoir of means to score and the statement made by their most defining trait: the art and heart and science of the comeback.

If New York is the city that never sleeps, Kansas City mayor Sly James would say, the Royals were symbolic of the city that never quits.

Forty times during the 2015 regular season, the Royals uncorked comebacks to win.

That proved just a preamble to the dream theme of the playoffs, in which they came from behind to win in a Major League Baseball-postseason record eight games — including all four World Series victories.

One way to understand that, per Baseball-Reference.com: The Mets led four of the five World Series games going into the eighth or ninth innings.

"MLB teams," it added, "lose three of those four games just once out of every 2,820 times."

There are a lot of potential explanations for that phenomenon, and fate and angels and luck maybe had some voice.

But a forensics test would reveal that it emanated from the DNA of this team, whose parts almost to a man are made up of those who have had to overcome in some way — and whose collective identity was forged by falling just short a year ago.

That romp to the 2014 World Series, you'll recall, was enabled by arguably the most unfathomable postseason comeback in MLB history, the rally to beat Oakland in the AL Wild Card Game after the Royals trailed 7-3 into the eighth inning.

The game was a portal to this new world order, one in which the fledgling Royals grew up overnight and won eight games in a row to get to a World Series that they came to expect to win.

When they didn't, there was no consolation in the idea of how far they'd come from the days of losing 100 games-plus four times in five years or all the slapstick stuff like having two outfielders run into the dugout as a ball dropped between them.

All they could think of was how far they still had to go.

That's why pitching coach Dave Eiland experienced "borderline depression" and third baseman Mike Moustakas felt no life in him for days and Jarrod Dyson stayed in the dugout and stared at the Giants celebrating and thought, "That's supposed to be us."

They set about making it so with a singlemindedness of purpose that began in spring training, infused by the seamless addition to the nucleus of a dozen new players — including Johnny Cueto and Ben Zobrist just before the trade deadline.

Then they accomplished it, through infinite pivotal moments and an infectious love for the game that enthralled Kansas City and created new admirers near and far.

They did it with fate and angels and luck lurking, yes, but they did it with something we can admire all the more: incredible talent fueled by unbreakable will that seemed to be a strong voice in their own fate.

— *Vahe Gregorian*

THE KANSAS CITY STAR

2/26/2015

It all starts here

AL champions have a title to defend this season, and a higher goal to shoot for

BY ANDY McCULLOUGH

SURPRISE, Ariz.
The residue from October resides in gold lettering on each of the 68 lockers inside the Royals' spring clubhouse. Just past 8 a.m. on Wednesday, first baseman Eric Hosmer stood in front of his cubicle. Behind him gleamed the title this club collected four months ago: American League champions.

"It gives you a certain swagger about your team," Hosmer said, "to know that you're defending something this coming year."

The events of last season restored the credibility of a long-dormant franchise, awakened a nation to the charms of an old-fashioned baseball club and buoyed the confidence of a group of players maturing into manhood.

On Wednesday morning, 119 days after the World Series ended and 40 days before opening day against the White Sox, the latest edition of the Royals gathered for its first full-squad workout. It was the start of a campaign the team hopes will end in champagne, rather than the tears of Oct. 29, 2014.

Wednesday's workout provided a panoply of the characters expected to star in the sequel: Hosmer, the budding leader; Alex Gordon, the homegrown hero approaching free agency; Lorenzo Cain, the breakout star of October; Yordano Ventura, the prospective ace; Greg Holland, Wade Davis and Kelvin Herrera, the relentless relief trio.

The industry casts doubt on their chances. The American League Central reloaded in impressive fashion. General manager Dayton Moore has said it could be baseball's toughest division. The road back to October will be pitted with potholes.

Bovada, the online gambling hub, set Kansas City's over-under for total victories at 79 1/2. PECOTA, the projection system of Baseball Prospectus, predicts 72 wins. The prognostications have caused eyes to roll within the Royals' clubhouse.

"Hearing that, you don't care about that, because that's just ridiculous," Hosmer said. "For whoever to make that prediction, to come in here and tell a bunch of guys who has been through an experience like last year, and went through a ride like that - to tell us we're going to win 72 games is just ridiculous."

Gordon offered one nettlesome reminder swept about by October's bliss. The Royals have never won the American League Central. Their division title drought still stretches back to 1985, when the Royals played in the Western Division.

"We still have a lot to prove," Gordon said. "You always hear about people predicting who is going to win the AL or who is going to win the Central. And, really, we're not on the list. You still have your doubters. But I think everyone in here still feels confident that we're going to make October."

Ned Yost is planning for the same result. When he and his staff mapped out this spring, they sought to ease their veteran players into action. During the first couple of weeks, the team may be more willing to use minor-leaguers in games. The calendar now must account for an extra month of work.

As the players settled down for breakfast, the drum machines and horns of Michael Jackson's "Wanna Be Startin' Somethin'" filled the air.

Yost called the group together after breakfast. He introduced his support staff to new faces such as outfielder Alex Rios, who occupies Billy Butler's old locker, and Kendrys Morales, who occupies Butler's old position at designated hitter. Yost veered into valedictory territory, praising the returnees for their performance in 2014, and challenging them to surpass it in 2015.

"Day one, let's try to have a fun one," Jarrod Dyson called out to all within earshot. Lorenzo Cain followed behind him, repeating a chorus, "We just get ready," culled from a B.o.B. single.

Cain burst into living rooms across the country with his performance in October. Dyson grabbed Cain and asked nearby photographers to capture the moment as he posed with "The MVP," a reference to Cain's award from the American League Championship Series. During the winter, the Royals said Cain emerged as the top jersey seller on the roster.

"Confidence is definitely through the roof right now," Cain said.

After stretching the pitchers departed for the back fields. The organization hopes the pitching trio of Ventura, Edinson Volquez and Danny Duffy can offset the departure of James Shields. Volquez filled the rotation's vacancy on a two-year contract. Duffy added 20 pounds of muscle in his quest to log 200 innings. But it is Ventura who will likely start opening day, who still inspires hyperbole from his contemporaries.

"The sky is the limit," Duffy said. "I think you're going to see some things this year that you've never seen before out of him."

Kansas City Royals (from left) Kendrys Morales, Salvador Perez, Eric Hosmer, Pedro Grifol and Jarrod Dyson before a spring training game against the Los Angeles Angels in Tempe, Ariz.

Kansas City Royals starting pitcher Edinson Volquez handed the ball to manager Ned Yost after giving up a walk during the Royals and Chicago Cubs spring training game at Surprise Stadium. Volquez was a key acquisition for the Royals who were hoping to fill the void left by the departure of last season's ace James Shields.

Kansas City Royals owner David Glass (left) talked with Royals manger Ned Yost and general manger Dayton Moore during morning workouts at Surprise Stadium in Surprise, Ariz.

Fantastic opener

Hot bats, solid pitching and good defense result in an easy victory over Chicago on opening day.

The Royals delivered a statement. On the same day they accepted their rings and hoisted the pennant, they drubbed the Chicago White Sox, a club favored to outpace them in 2015.

Yordano Ventura exited midway through the seventh, but only after he stymied his guests for six innings without much difficulty. The rest of the day unfolded in idyllic fashion: Alcides Escobar excelled at the top of the batting order. Mike Moustakas launched the first opposite-field homer of his career. Kendrys Morales reached base four times and scored twice. Alex Rios lifted a three-run homer in the seventh, capping a three-hit day.

And those were only the newer ingredients. The old elements still applied. The outfielders raced down any fly balls foolish enough to exhibit hang time, while the infielders converted double plays and leaped to snag line drives. The bullpen logged three scoreless innings.

"There were just so many story lines in that game," Ned Yost said. "For our players coming back, getting their rings and then putting on a great performance in front of a sold-out crowd."

– Andy McCullough

April

CENTRAL	W	L	Pct	GB	RS	RA	L10	Str
Detroit	15	7	.682	—	107	90	5-5	W1
Kansas City	14	7	.667	½	111	73	6-4	L1
Chicago	8	10	.444	5	62	77	5-5	L1
Minnesota	9	12	.429	5½	74	98	5-5	L1
Cleveland	7	13	.350	7	78	93	3-7	W1

SCHEDULE

Date	Opponent	Result	Record
4/6	White Sox	W 10-1	1-0
4/8	White Sox	W 7-5	2-0
4/9	White Sox	W 4-1	3-0
4/10	at Angels	W 4-2	4-0
4/11	at Angels	W 6-4	5-0
4/12	at Angels	W 9-2	6-0
4/13	at Twins	W 12-3	7-0
4/15	at Twins	L 1-3	7-1
4/16	at Twins	L 5-8	7-2
4/17	Athletics	W 6-4	8-2
4/18	Athletics	L 0-5	8-3
4/19	Athletics	W 4-2	9-3
4/20	Twins	W 7-1	10-3
4/21	Twins	W 6-5	11-3
4/22	Twins	L 0-3	11-4
4/23	at White Sox	W 3-2	12-4
4/24	at White Sox	L 2-3	12-5
4/25	at White Sox	Postponed	12-5
4/26	at White Sox	L 2-3	12-5
4/26	at White Sox	L 3-5	12-6
4/27	at Indians	W 6-2	13-6
4/28	at Indians	W 11-5	14-6
4/29	at Indians	L 5-7	14-7
4/30	Tigers	W 8-1	15-7

Straight outta Kauffman

APRIL 6: Baseball teams play about 1,450 innings per season, and in the fifth inning of the Royals' 2015 season, the bad blood started. Lorenzo Cain was plunked by a Jeff Samardzija pitch that Cain said was intentional. The Royals won 10-1, but with just 0.003 percent of their season gone, the tone was set.

APRIL 15: Royals lose 3-1 at Minnesota and Eric Hosmer sagely notes, "The perfect season is gone."

APRIL 17: Oakland's Brett Lawrie made a hard slide into second base that caught little of the bag and a lot of Royals shortstop Alcides Escobar. Tempers flared, but there was no altercation ...

APRIL 18: Lawrie said he texted Escobar to apologize, but it apparently went to a different Alcides Escobar, because the Royals shortstop never heard from Lawrie. Lawrie, however, heard from Yordano Ventura, who plunked him. The A's, who won 5-0, called this "bush league."

APRIL 19: There was one batter hit in the finale to the Royals-A's three-game set: Lorenzo Cain. Kelvin Herrera threw a 100-mph pitch behind Lawrie and was ejected. Herrera pointed to his head while leaving the field and the nation's opinion of the Royals, particularly on the West Coast, was not positive. The Royals won 4-2.

APRIL 23: Remember Jeff Samardzija? He was ejected from this day's Royals-White Sox game even though he didn't pitch. Chris Sale plunked Mike Moustakas and fisticuffs ensued. Sale even attempted to enter the Royals' clubhouse later to, uh, discuss his differences. The nation's opinion of the Royals, particularly in Chicago, was not positive. The Royals won 3-2 in 13 innings.

JOHN SLEEZER

This is the hit-by-pitch that got Ned Yost ejected on April 19. Lorenzo Cain was plunked by A's starter Scott Kazmir.

JOHN SLEEZER

Manager Ned Yost got his money's worth after getting kicked out of the Royals' April 19 game against Oakland.

May

STANDINGS May 31, 2015

CENTRAL	W	L	Pct	GB	RS	RA	L10	Str
Kansas City	29	18	.617	—	223	173	6-4	W1
Minnesota	29	19	.604	½	219	199	8-2	W1
Detroit	28	22	.560	2½	206	203	5-5	L2
Chicago	22	26	.458	7½	173	221	4-6	L1
Cleveland	22	26	.458	7½	515	215	7-3	L1

SCHEDULE

Date	Opponent	Result	Record
5/1	Tigers	● W 4-1	16-7
5/2	Tigers	L 1-2	16-8
5/3	Tigers	L 4-6	16-9
5/5	Indians	● W 5-3	17-9
5/6	Indians	L 3-10	17-10
5/7	Indians	● W 7-4	18-10
5/8	at Tigers	L 5-6	18-11
5/9	at Tigers	● W 6-2	19-11
5/10	at Tigers	● W 2-1	20-11
5/11	at Rangers	L 2-8	20-12
5/12	at Rangers	● W 7-6	21-12
5/13	at Rangers	L 2-5	21-13
5/14	at Rangers	● W 6-3	22-13
5/15	Yankees	● W 12-1	23-13
5/16	Yankees	L 1-5	23-14
5/17	Yankees	● W 6-0	24-14
5/19	Reds	● W 3-0	25-14
5/20	Reds	● W 7-1	26-14
5/22	Cardinals	● W 5-0	27-14
5/23	Cardinals	● W 3-2	28-14
5/24	Cardinals	L 1-6	28-15
5/25	at Yankees	L 1-14	28-16
5/26	at Yankees	L 1-5	28-17
5/27	at Yankees	L 2-4	28-18
5/29	at Cubs	● W 8-4	29-18
5/30	at Cubs	Postponed	29-18
5/31	at Cubs	L 1-2	29-19

Hey! Is that Hoch?

MAY 7: Welcome back, Luke. In his first appearance in 585 days, Luke Hochevar made a triumphant return from Tommy John surgery by pitching a scoreless inning of relief as the Royals beat the Indians 7-4.

MAY 8: Jason Vargas was placed on the disabled list because of a flexor strain and Mike Moustakas left because of a family emergency and was placed on the bereavement list.

MAY 13: Catcher Salvador Perez offered a suggestion for a pitch that Yordano Ventura shook off. Ventura's pitch of choice was then hit out of the park for a home run by Shin-Soo Choo and the Rangers went on to beat the Royals 5-2.

MAY 23: Mother Nature is a Royals fan. Well, for one day, at least. Edinson Volquez pitched the entire game as the Royals won 3-2 when the game was called in the bottom of the sixth inning because of rain.

MAY 26: In the first update of All-Star Game voting, five Royals led at their respective positions, drawing still more scorn from fans across the nation, who have no idea how much worse it will get.

MAY 29: "Let's Go Royals" chants were heard for possibly the first time at Wrigley Field. The Royals scored four runs in seven innings against Jake Arrieta, who would go on to be in the Cy Young race in the National League this year. They piled it on against the Cubs' bullpen and won a potential World Series matchup 8-4.

AP PHOTO/LM OTERO

Catcher Salvador Perez (right) tries to calm down starting pitcher Yordano Ventura during the game against the Texas Rangers on Wednesday, May 13, 2015.

JOHN SLEEZER

"It feels great to be back, to really be a contributor and not just be a bona fide fan in the dugout," Luke Hochevar said.

June

STANDINGS June 30, 2015

CENTRAL	W	L	Pct	GB	RS	RA	L10	Str
Kansas City	44	29	.603	—	317	264	6-4	L1
Minnesota	40	36	.526	5½	320	320	4-6	L2
Detroit	39	36	.520	6	327	330	5-5	W2
Cleveland	34	41	.453	11	298	331	3-7	W1
Chicago	32	42	.432	12½	257	338	4-6	L2

SCHEDULE

Date	Opponent	Result	Record
6/2	Indians	L 1-2	29-20
6/3	Indians	● W 4-2	30-20
6/4	Indians	L 2-6	30-21
6/5	Rangers	L 0-4	30-22
6/6	Rangers	L 2-4	30-23
6/7	Rangers	● W 4-3	31-23
6/8	at Twins	● W 3-1	32-23
6/9	at Twins	● W 2-0	33-23
6/10	at Twins	● W 7-2	34-23
6/12	at Cardinals	L 0-4	34-24
6/13	at Cardinals	L 2-3	34-25
6/14	at Cardinals	Postponed	34-25
6/15	at Brewers	● W 8-5	35-25
6/16	at Brewers	● W 7-2	36-25
6/17	Brewers	● W 10-2	37-25
6/18	Brewers	● W 3-2	38-25
6/19	Red Sox	L 3-7	38-26
6/20	Red Sox	● W 7-4	39-26
6/21	Red Sox	L 2-13	39-27
6/22	at Mariners	● W 4-1	40-27
6/23	at Mariners	L 0-7	40-28
6/24	at Mariners	● W 8-2	41-28
6/26	at Athletics	● W 5-2	42-28
6/27	at Athletics	● W 3-2	43-28
6/28	at Athletics	● W 5-3	44-28
6/29	at Astros	L 1-6	44-29
6/30	at Astros	L 0-4	44-30

Ned's club record

JUNE 2: Wade Davis gave up a run for the first time this season, but it was the umpires' fault. The Royals turned a double play in the eighth inning, but Cleveland's Jose Ramirez was ruled safe at first. A replay challenge upheld the call and the Indians scored the go-ahead run and won 2-1. The next day, Major League Baseball told Royals manager Ned Yost that it had botched the replay.

JUNE 8: Seven Royals were leading at their positions for the All-Star Game. Only Houston second baseman Jose Altuve and Angels outfielder Mike Trout were keeping it from being a Royals sweep.

JUNE 10: David Price was stunned that the Royals are dominating the All-Star Game voting, so he tweeted out his support for fans to vote for Miguel Cabrera: "please do something about the Allstate voting ... not that's it's funny but it's kind of a joke." We all assumed he meant All-Star voting.

JUNE 16: Since the dawn of the designated hitter, no Royals pitcher had tallied three RBIs in a game. But Chris Young accomplished the feat and tossed seven shutout innings at Milwaukee as the Royals won 7-2.

JUNE 18: Champagne showers are usually reserved for October, but Ned Yost was doused with Dom Perignon following a 3-2 win in Milwaukee after getting his 411th win as the team's manager, a new club record.

JUNE 28: Salvador Perez's 500th career hit was a home run as the Royals beat the A's 5-3 and finished the sweep. Alas, the Royals were unable to find the ball to return it to Perez as a keepsake.

JOHN SLEEZER

Salvador Perez homered for his 500th career hit. Was that how he dreamed it up? Perez grinned from ear to ear. "One hundred percent."

JOHN SLEEZER

Ned Yost is now the winningest manager in Royals history after beating Milwaukee 3-2 on June 18 to sweep the series with the Brewers.

July

CENTRAL	W	L	Pct	GB	RS	RA	L10	Str
Kansas City	61	40	.604	—	434	372	6-4	L2
Minnesota	52	48	.520	8½	424	423	2-8	L4
Detroit	50	52	.490	11½	455	488	4-6	W2
Chicago	49	51	.490	11½	366	418	7-3	L1
Cleveland	46	54	.460	14½	392	430	3-7	W1

SCHEDULE

Date	Opponent	Result	Record
7/1	at Astros	L 5-6	44-31
7/2	Twins	L 0-2	44-32
7/3	Twins	● W 3-2	45-32
7/4	Twins	L 3-5	45-33
7/5	Twins	● W 3-2	46-33
7/6	Rays	Postponed	46-33
7/7	Rays	W 9-5	47-33
7/7	Rays	● W 7-1	48-33
7/8	Rays	● W 9-7	49-33
7/9	Rays	● W 8-3	50-33
7/10	Blue Jays	● W 3-0	51-33
7/11	Blue Jays	L 2-6	51-34
7/12	Blue Jays	● W 11-10	52-34
7/17	at White Sox	● W 4-2	53-34
7/17	at White Sox	L 0-2	53-35
7/18	at White Sox	● W 7-6	54-35
7/19	at White Sox	● W 4-1	55-35
7/20	Pirates	L 7-10	55-36
7/21	Pirates	● W 3-1	56-36
7/22	Pirates	● W 5-1	57-36
7/23	at Cardinals	L 3-4	57-37
7/24	Astros	L 0-4	57-38
7/25	Astros	● W 2-1	58-38
7/26	Astros	● W 5-1	59-38
7/27	at Indians	● W 9-4	60-38
7/28	at Indians	● W 2-1	61-38
7/29	at Indians	L 1-12	61-39
7/30	at Blue Jays	L 2-5	61-40
7/31	at Blue Jays	L 6-7	61-41

The stars of summer

JULY 5: All-Star voting, a source of angst for baseball fans everywhere but Kansas City, netted a franchise-record four starters for the Royals: Alex Gordon, Lorenzo Cain, Alcides Escobar and Salvador Perez. Pitchers Kelvin Herrera and Wade Davis are selected for the AL team by All-Star manager Ned Yost.

JULY 8: More than 28,000 fans at Kauffman Stadium fell completely silent after Alex Gordon crumpled to the ground while chasing a fly ball. A groin injury forced him from the game and put him on the disabled list for eight weeks.

JULY 10: Mike Moustakas won the fan vote for the All-Star Game and he left his ailing mother, at her request, to get to Cincinnati for the Midsummer Classic.

JULY 21: One day after allowing six runs on 10 hits in four innings, Yordano Ventura was optioned to Class AAA Omaha ... but fate intervened. Before heading up I-29, Ventura was told not to go because Jason Vargas left his start against the Pirates early with an arm injury. He would need Tommy John surgery and Ventura's trip to Nebraska was canceled.

JULY 26: After years of watching other teams acquire star players ahead of the trade deadline, the Royals swooped in and made a huge deal, getting Johnny Cueto from the Reds.

JULY 28: This was the most significant day of the season. In the afternoon, the Royals traded for Oakland infielder/outfielder Ben Zobrist, who was coveted by a dozen other teams. That night, they held off Cleveland 2-1 behind an incredible ninth-inning play by Omar Infante and Alcides Escobar, who turned a 4-6-3 putout. After the game, the Royals started dropping the numbers 17 and 38 into interviews. This was based on Lorenzo Cain's walk-up song, "Trap Queen," by rapper Fetty Wap and Remy Boyz 1738. Meanwhile, Indians starter Trevor Bauer ripped Royals fans on Twitter. Quite a day, indeed.

JOHN SLEEZER

The Royals entered July with a 4 ½-game lead on the Minnesota Twins and entered August with an eight-game advantage after finishing the month 17-11. In between they lost outfielder Alex Gordon to a groin strain and also picked up two key trade pieces in Johnny Cueto and Ben Zobrist.

JOHN SLEEZER

Royals pitchers Jason Vargas (left) and Yordano Ventura (right) watched from the dugout during the game against the Pittsburgh Pirates on July 22.

August

SCHEDULE

Date	Opponent	Result	Record
8/1	at Blue Jays	● W 7-6	62-41
8/2	at Blue Jays	L 2-5	62-42
8/4	at Tigers	● W 5-1	63-42
8/5	at Tigers	L 1-2	63-43
8/6	at Tigers	L 6-8	63-44
8/7	White Sox	● W 3-2	64-44
8/8	White Sox	● W 7-6	65-44
8/9	White Sox	● W 5-4	66-44
8/10	Tigers	● W 4-0	67-44
8/11	Tigers	● W 6-1	68-44
8/12	Tigers	L 4-7	68-45
8/13	Angels	L 6-7	68-46
8/14	Angels	● W 4-1	69-46
8/15	Angels	● W 9-4	70-46
8/16	Angels	● W 4-3	71-46
8/18	at Reds	● W 3-1	72-46
8/19	at Reds	● W 4-3	73-46
8/20	at Red Sox	L 1-4	73-47
8/21	at Red Sox	L 2-7	73-48
8/22	at Red Sox	● W 6-3	74-48
8/23	at Red Sox	● W 8-6	75-48
8/24	Orioles	● W 8-3	76-48
8/25	Orioles	● W 3-2	77-48
8/26	Orioles	L 5-8	77-49
8/27	Orioles	● W 5-3	78-49
8/28	at Rays	● W 3-2	79-49
8/29	at Rays	● W 6-3	80-49
8/30	at Rays	L 2-3	80-50

Hot and ready

AUG. 2: This was the day the Royals-Blue Jays rivalry was born. Toronto won 5-2, but the Blue Jays were incensed that the Royals pitched inside to their batters. Josh Donaldson was hit by one pitch and nearly plunked by another. Afterward, Royals starter Edinson Volquez said Donaldson was "crying like a little baby." Troy Tulowitzki was also hit, and both benches were warned. When Alcides Escobar was hit, Toronto's Aaron Sanchez was ejected.

AUG. 8: The Royals beat the White Sox 7-6 at Kauffman Stadium for a 10½-game lead over the Twins in the AL Central, their first double-digit division lead since 1980.

AUG. 10: Welcome to KC, Johnny. In his first start at Kauffman Stadium, Johnny Cueto tossed a four-hit shutout as the Royals beat the Tigers 4-0. It was the stuff of legend, and fans dreamed of Cueto dominating in the postseason.

AUG. 13: The unthinkable happened. The Royals led the Angels 5-1 after seven innings. Game over, right? Well, Wade Davis allowed two runs in the eighth and Greg Holland failed to get an out in the ninth inning, allowing four runs as the Angels won 7-6.

AUG. 19: The Royals swept a two-game series in Cincinnati, winning 4-3 and picking up their 73rd win of the season. That's significant because it was one more than Baseball Prospectus' projection system predicted for the Royals in 2015.

JOHN SLEEZER

Royals fans of recent vintage were accustomed to seeing their club shed talent at the trade deadline, not add reinforcements. They did the latter in adding ace Johnny Cueto.

JOHN SLEEZER

Ben Zobrist proved to be the most impactful of the Royals' new faces. He can reliably play any position in the field and brought dependability to the plate as a switch-hitter with some power.

September

STANDINGS October 4, 2015

CENTRAL	W	L	Pct	GB	RS	RA	L10	Str
Kansas City	95	67	.586	–	724	641	6-4	W5
Minnesota	83	79	.512	12	696	700	5-5	L3
Cleveland	81	80	.503	13½	669	640	6-4	W3
Chicago	76	86	.469	19	622	701	4-6	L1
Detroit	74	87	.460	20½	689	803	4-6	W1

SCHEDULE

Date	Opponent	Result	Record
9/1	Tigers	L 5-6	80-51
9/2	Tigers	W 12-1	81-51
9/3	Tigers	W 15-7	82-51
9/4	White Sox	L 1-12	82-52
9/5	White Sox	L 1-6	82-53
9/6	White Sox	L 5-7	82-54
9/7	Twins	L 2-6	82-55
9/8	Twins	W 4-2	83-55
9/9	Twins	L 2-3	83-56
9/11	at Orioles	L 8-14	83-57
9/12	at Orioles	W 14-6	84-57
9/13	at Orioles	L 2-8	84-58
9/14	at Indians	L 3-8	84-59
9/15	at Indians	W 2-0	85-59
9/16	at Indians	L 1-5	85-60
9/17	at Indians	W 8-4	86-60
9/18	at Tigers	L 4-5	86-61
9/19	at Tigers	L 5-6	86-62
9/20	at Tigers	W 10-3	87-62
9/22	Mariners	L 2-11	87-63
9/23	Mariners	W 4-3	88-63
9/24	Mariners	W 10-4	89-63
9/25	Indians	L 0-6	89-64
9/26	Indians	L 5-9	89-65
9/27	Indians	W 3-0	90-65
9/28	at Cubs	L 0-1	90-66
9/29	at White Sox	L 2-4	90-67
9/30	at White Sox	W 5-3	91-67
10/1	at White Sox	W 6-4	92-67
10/2	at Twins	W 3-1	93-67
10/3	at Twins	W 5-1	94-67
10/4	at Twins	W 6-1	95-67

Slump... what slump?

SEPT. 1: Alex Gordon was re-activated after being on the disabled list since July 8 with a severe groin strain.

SEPT. 12: Mike Moustakas hit two homers and set a franchise record with nine RBIs as the Royals won 14-6. After the game, a Clydesdale horse born at an Anheuser-Busch barn in Boonville, Mo., was named Moose. Moustakas later said in an interview that his mother had died in August.

SEPT. 15: Alex Rios hit a solo home run in Cleveland as the Royals won 2-0. A surprising thing happened as Rios rounded the bases, though: fireworks went off over the Indians' stadium. The guy in charge of the pyrotechnics later said he felt really, really, really bad about the mistake.

SEPT. 17: Omar Infante, who had been relegated to the bench because of his troubles at the plate, broke out with seven RBIs in an 8-4 win at Cleveland. It would have tied the franchise record for most RBIs in a game, but Moose had that big game just a few days earlier.

SEPT. 19: The Royals announced that Omar Infante had a strained oblique and could miss the start of the playoffs.

SEPT. 22: Ned Yost announced that Wade Davis would be the closer for the rest of the season. Davis took the place of Greg Holland, who was experiencing elbow tightness.

SEPT. 24: The Royals beat the Mariners 10-4 and, combined with a Twins loss, clinched the AL Central Division for the first time and won a division for the first time since 1985.

JOHN SLEEZER

Closer Greg Holland won't be joining the Royals' relief corps this postseason after undergoing surgery on Friday to repair ligament damage in his throwing elbow. He was one of the stars of last season's "HDH Bullpen."

Royals catcher Salvador Perez (left) and third baseman Mike Moustakas were dunked with ice water after the 10-4 victory over the Seattle Mariners that clinched the AL Central Division on September 24 at Kauffman Stadium. After slumping for most of the month of September, the Royals finished strong, winning their last five games to secure home-field advantage throughout the playoffs.

JOHN SLEEZER

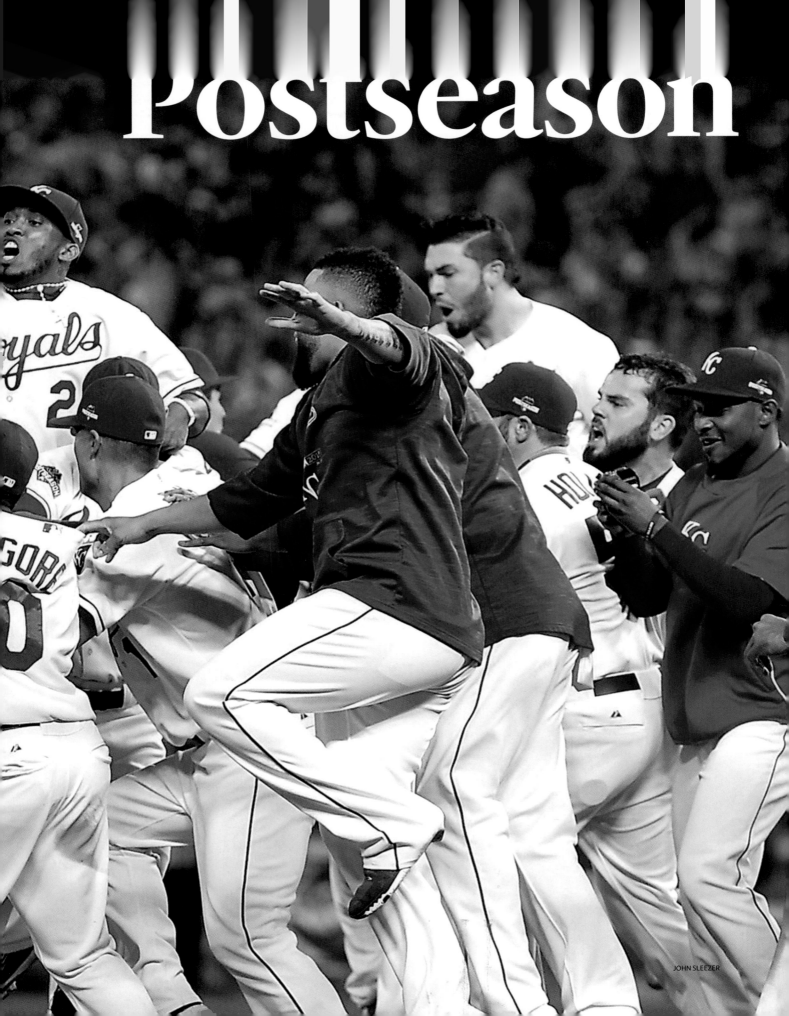

Postseason

Royals catcher Salvador Perez watched glumly as Houston's Colby Rasmus celebrated a home run in the eighth inning of Thursday's ALDS Game 1 at Kauffman Stadium.

JOE LEDFORD

		1 2 3	4 5 6	7 8 9		R	H	E
ALDS GAME 1	Houston	2 1 0	0 1 0	0 1 0	—	5	11	0
	Kansas City	0 1 0	1 0 0	0 0 0	—	2	6	0

 L (2) (3) (4) (5)

THE KANSAS CITY STAR

10/9/2015

Mood killer

Starting pitcher Yordano Ventura gives up three runs in two innings

Kendrys Morales hits two homers in a losing cause

BY ANDY McCULLOUGH

Silence no longer suits Kauffman Stadium, not after the Kansas City exorcism of the 2014 playoffs and the season-long euphoria of 2015. This ballpark saw the Royals raise a pennant last year and raise a division title last month.

Yet silence, the collective stifling of more than 40,000 voices ready to roar during Game 1 of the American League Division Series, radiated through the park in the final moments of a 5-2 loss to the Astros.

The fans frothed with anticipation when the Royals, at last, placed two runners aboard in the bottom of the eighth against lefty reliever Oliver Perez. The descent of Eric Hosmer's pop-up in foul territory operated like a light switch. The noise ceased, and the Royals turned to today, when they can even this series.

Facing a distorted mirror image of themselves - a youthful team stocked with athleticism and plunging into October for the first time - the Royals came undone in the face of Houston's crafty defensive positioning and offensive firepower. Kansas City managed only six hits.

"We just really couldn't get anything going, outside of Kendrys," Hosmer said. "Didn't really get anybody on in the beginning of an inning. Couldn't really get something going. When we did (in) a couple of innings, just couldn't get the big hit."

So now, the defending American League champions and owners of the league's best record this year, will turn to Johnny Cueto for Game 2 this afternoon. He faces lefty Scott Kazmir, a season-long antagonist for the Royals.

On Thursday night, Kansas City's plans fizzled from the start. The Royals intended for Yordano Ventura to bully the Astros with his fastball. Instead he yielded three runs in two innings and departed after a 49-minute rain delay interrupted the night.

Pitching only three days after his father's memorial service, Chris Young provided four innings of one-run emergency relief. Ryan Madson allowed a homer by outfielder Colby Rasmus in the eighth.

The effort from Young kept Kansas City within striking distance. With two solo shots, Kendrys Morales became the first Royal to hit multiple homers in a playoff game since George Brett in the 1985 American League Championship Series. The rest of the bunch managed only two hits in six innings against Astros starter Collin McHugh.

"He was really good tonight," Royals shortstop Alcides Escobar said. "He was throwing a lot of cutters. He's down and away. He mixes with the curveball. He's throwing really good."

The organization bucked expectations in setting their playoff rotation. Instead of Cueto, the ace the team acquired in July, the Royals deemed Ventura their Game 1 starter. The decision arose from Kansas City's confidence in Ventura and Cueto's reluctance to pitch on short rest, as he would have needed to for Thursday.

JOHN SLEEZER

After a 49-minute rain delay, Chris Young took the mound in relief of Yordano Ventura. Young settled down the Astros with seven strikeouts in four innings.

Ventura did not author an auspicious start. He could not record an out until his 20th pitch. By then, the Astros had already loaded the bases thanks to a single by second baseman Jose Altuve, a walk by outfielder George Springer and a single by shortstop Carlos Correa. Rasmus drove in a run with a ground-out, and designated hitter Evan Gattis soon did the same. The inning lasted 13 minutes and required 24 pitches from Ventura.

An inning later, Astros outfielder Jake Marisnick whacked an 0-2, 99-mph fastball to the wall for a two-out double. Up came Altuve, the pint-sized former batting champion. One Royals official compared him to Yogi Berra, famous for both his lack of size and his ability to transform pitches outside the zone into base hits. Altuve soon smacked a fastball into right field.

As the ball hit the grass, Alex Rios charged forward. He

clutched twice before he threw. Marisnick sprinted from second base and spotted the whirling arm of third-base coach Gary Pettis. The throw from Rios arrived too late and the deficit expanded to three.

The park felt a jolt in the bottom of the inning, when McHugh tried to sneak a fastball past Morales' hands. In his first postseason at-bat since 2009, Morales hooked a homer down the right-field line.

Actual lightning followed the metaphorical thunder. Salvador Perez never received a chance to crouch behind the plate for the third inning. The grounds crew unfurled the tarp, and the delay evicted Ventura from the premises.

Houston stuck with McHugh. He retired the side without incident in the third. In the fourth, he flipped a lazy change-up over the heart of the plate. Morales tattooed the pitch, high and deep, a parabola that cleared the right-field fence.

The Royals turned to Young. He had not pitched in the playoffs since the fall of 2006, when he posted a victory for San Diego after nearly seven scoreless innings against

St. Louis, back before he underwent the succession of shoulder surgeries that altered his career.

Called into relief, Young struck out the side in the third and the fourth. With one out in the fifth, he yielded a homer to Springer on an elevated, 88-mph fastball. The solo shot could have been worse: Just moments earlier, Perez threw out Altuve, his childhood friend, trying to steal second.

Young waded through the Astros lineup through the sixth inning. The Astros kept McHugh in the game. He had benefited from stellar defense all evening. Altuve snagged a sizzling liner off Lorenzo Cain's bat in the fourth. Marisnick dived to rob Escobar of a hit with two runners aboard in the fifth.

In six at-bats against Cain and Hosmer, the two prime generators of Royals offense, McHugh recorded six outs. Houston manager A.J. Hinch allowed McHugh to face Morales with two outs in the sixth.

The gamble went unpunished. Morales floated a fly ball into the glove of Springer in right field. The park again went quiet.

ASTROS 5, ROYALS 2

Houston	AB	R	H	BI	BB	SO	Avg.
Altuve 2b	5	1	3	1	0	0	.600
Springer rf	4	2	1	1	1	1	.500
Correa ss	5	0	1	0	0	2	.200
Col.Rasmus lf	3	1	1	2	1	1	.333
Gattis dh	4	0	1	1	0	1	.250
1-C.Gomez pr-dh	0	0	0	0	0	0	---
Valbuena 3b	3	0	0	0	1	3	.000
Carter 1b	4	0	1	0	0	2	.250
Ma.Gonzalez 1b	0	0	0	0	0	0	---
J.Castro c	4	0	0	0	0	3	.000
Marisnick cf	4	1	2	0	0	1	.500
Totals	36	5	11	5	3	14	

Kansas City	AB	R	H	BI	BB	SO	Avg.
A.Escobar ss	4	0	0	0	0	1	.000
Zobrist 2b	4	0	2	0	0	0	.500
L.Cain cf	4	0	1	0	0	0	.250
Hosmer 1b	4	0	0	0	0	0	.000
K.Morales dh	4	2	2	2	0	1	.500
Moustakas 3b	3	0	0	0	0	0	.000
S.Perez c	4	0	0	0	0	1	.000
A.Gordon lf	4	0	1	0	0	0	.250
Rios rf	2	0	0	0	1	1	.000
Totals	33	2	6	2	1	4	

Houston	210	010	010	—	5 11 0
Kansas City	010	100	000	—	2 6 0

1-ran for Gattis in the 8th.
LOB: Houston 7, Kansas City 6. **2B:** Marisnick (1). **HR:** Springer (1), off C.Young; Col.Rasmus (1), off Madson; K.Morales 2 (2), off McHugh 2. **RBIs:** Altuve (1), Springer (1), Col.Rasmus 2 (2), Gattis (1), K.Morales 2 (2). **SB:** Col.Rasmus (1), Zobrist (1). **CS:** Altuve (1).
Runners left in scoring position: Houston 5 (Valbuena 2, Springer, J.Castro, Correa); Kansas City 3 (Hosmer 2, Zobrist). **RISP:** Houston 2 for 10; Kansas City 0 for 5. **Runners moved up:** Altuve, Col.Rasmus, Gattis. **GIDP:** J.Castro 1. **DP:** Kansas City 1 (Zobrist, A.Escobar, Hosmer).

Houston	IP	H	R	ER	BB	SO	NP	ERA
McHugh W, 1-0	6	4	2	2	1	1	92	3.00
Sipp	1	0	0	0	0	0	17	0.00
W.Harris	⅔	2	0	0	1	1	17	0.00
O.Perez	⅓	0	0	0	0	0	3	0.00
Gregerson S, 1	1	0	0	0	0	2	13	0.00

Kansas City	IP	H	R	ER	BB	SO	NP	ERA
Ventura L, 0-1	2	4	3	3	1	2	42	13.50
C.Young	4	3	1	1	2	7	70	2.25
K.Herrera	1	1	0	0	2	1	12	0.00
Madson	1	2	1	1	0	3	16	9.00
Hochevar	1	1	0	0	0	1	11	0.00

Holds: Harris (1), O.Perez (1), Sipp (1).
Inherited runners-scored: O.Perez 2-0.
HBP: by Gregerson (Moustakas).
Umpires: Home, Lance Barksdale; First, Angel Hernandez; Second, Mike Everitt; Third, Ron Kulpa; Left, Gerry Davis; Right, Todd Tichenor. **Time:** 3:14 (Delay: 0:49). **Att:** 40,146.

HOW THEY SCORED

ASTROS FIRST: Altuve led off and singled to left. Springer walked. Correa singled to right, Altuve to third, Springer to second. Rasmus grounded out to second, Altuve scored, Springer to third, Correa to second. Gattis grounded out to shortstop, Springer scored. Astros 2, Royals 0.

ASTROS SECOND: With two outs, Marisnick doubled to left center. Altuve singled to right, Marisnick scored. Astros 3, Royals 0.

ROYALS SECOND: Morales led off and homered to right. Astros 3, Royals 1.

ROYALS FOURTH: With two outs, Morales homered to right. Astros 3, Royals 2.

ASTROS FIFTH: With one out, Springer homered to left center. Astros 4, Royals 2.

ASTROS EIGHTH: Rasmus led off and homered to right center. Astros 5, Royals 2.

TAMMY LJUNGBLAD

Frustration showed on the face of Royals left fielder Alex Gordon after a home run by Houston's George Springer flew over his head in the fifth inning of Thursday's ALDS game at Kauffman Stadium.

TAMMY LJUNGBLAD

JILL TOYOSHIBA

The Astros padded their lead in the eigth inning Thursday with a solo home run by left fielder Colby Rasmus (center). He bashed a pitch off Royals reliever Ryan Madson.

Up and away, twice

Morales' two blasts aren't enough

Designated hitter Kendrys Morales did his part at the plate in Game 1 of the ALDS, becoming the first Royal since George Brett to homer two times in one playoff game.

On a night in which the offense was muted by Astros starter Collin McHugh, Morales offered the only hints of life. In the bottom of the second, Morales, a veteran designated hitter, sat on a 2-1 fastball and yanked the offering inside the right-field foul pole. The ball landed in the seats in right field, sending Kauffman Stadium into a frenzy, and the Royals had cut the Astros' lead to 3-1.

Two innings later, Morales went to work on McHugh once more, taking a thunderous hack on a 1-1 change-up and sending the baseball deep into the night. The solo shot pulled the Royals to within 3-2 in the bottom of the fourth. And that was that. The offense would go silent the rest of the night. Morales' two swings were the only offense the Royals could muster.

- Rustin Dodd

JILL TOYOSHIBA

Royals third baseman Mike Moustakas was frustrated after he grounded out in the seventh inning. He didn't have any of the Royals' six hits.

Royals first baseman Eric Hosmer connected for a single that drove in the Royals' first run during a two-run sixth inning.

DAVID EULITT

ALDS GAME 2

	1 2 3	4 5 6	7 8 9	R	H	E
Houston	121	000	000 —	4	8	0
Kansas City	010	100	210 —	5	11	0

THE KANSAS CITY STAR

10/10/2015

Fit to be tied

Alcides Escobar takes advantage of Astros' outfield positioning with a triple

Ben Zobrist follows with a single for go-ahead run in Royals' 5-4 win

BY ANDY McCULLOUGH

The baseball hung in the sky for a lifetime, floating like a horsehide-covered offering to the Baseball Gods who had been so cruel to the Royals for the first 15 innings of the American League Division Series.

Ned Yost often jokes about the talismanic powers of Alcides Escobar as the Royals' leadoff hitter, but in the seventh inning of a series-tying, stress-reducing, mojo-restoring 5-4 victory over the Astros, the Royals experienced a genuine bit of magic.

"I'm not sure what happened," center fielder Lorenzo Cain said. "I'm just happy it fell."

A two-run deficit erased and a must-win game tied heading into the final innings, Escobar pounced on a first-pitch cutter from Astros reliever Will Harris. His drive drifted into a Bermuda Triangle between center fielder Jake Marisnick and right fielder George Springer. The two fleet-footed defenders sprinted through bits of sun and shadow, only to watch the baseball land in the grass of Kauffman Stadium.

DAVID EULITT

Johnny Cueto was rocky early, tossing 49 pitches through two innings, but settled down later in the game.

Escobar sprinted all the way to third, a "game-changing play," third baseman Mike Moustakas said. The triple sent the crowd, unnerved by a Game 1 defeat and wounded by Johnny Cueto's dispiriting start earlier in the day, into hysterics. A go-ahead single by Ben Zobrist only heightened the volume.

Zobrist pumped his fist as he ran to first base, an exhortation to his teammates and a reminder to his opponents: Houston, we have a series.

"Down 0-1 in a series, we're not panicking or anything," Moustakas said. "We're going to go out there and try to find a way to win. And we did that today."

Cueto survived a rocky opening to throw six innings of four-run baseball. Cueto did not resemble an ace, but he kept his club within range. And his teammates eventually broke through against the Houston bullpen, with a two-run rally in the sixth. Salvador Perez hit a solo homer in the second and collected a bases-loaded walk in the sixth to tie the game.

"Today's one of those games where a guy like Johnny Cueto earns his name," Eric Hosmer said before the game. "We need him to step up for us today."

Cueto could not deliver. He retired second baseman Jose Altuve with the game's first pitch, but walked Springer. Two batters later, Colby Rasmus fished for an ankle-high change-up. He walloped an RBI double over Alex Rios' head in right field.

The second inning vexed Cueto with bad luck. His third pitch of the inning shattered the bat of first baseman Chris Carter. A single still fell in left field. Cueto picked up two strikes on catcher Jason Castro, then found himself at the mercy of umpire Angel Hernandez.

At 0-2, Cueto fired a high cutter in search of the outside corner. Hernandez deemed it a ball. He did the same with a fastball low and away. Cueto missed with four consecutive fastballs and cutters. Castro took first base.

Up came Marisnick. He tried to sacrifice himself with a bunt. The Royals would not oblige. Moustakas scooped up the ball as Escobar raced to cover him at the third-base bag. Cueto pointed toward third, which caused Moustakas to turn and see there was no play. By the time he threw to first, Marisnick was safe.

With two on, Cueto busted Springer inside with a 93-mph fastball. Springer still floated a two-run single into left.

"In the beginning, he didn't feel as strong," Royals coach Pedro Grifol said. "But then he was able to settle down and locate. And obviously, some of the balls that they hit, fell."

The Royals shaved a run off the deficit in the bottom of the second. Perez detonated a belt-high cutter from Astros starter

Scott Kazmir. Perez parked the solo blast in the Royals' bullpen in left field.

The crowd did not have long to enjoy the moment. In the next inning, Cueto served up a solo homer to Rasmus. This time, Rasmus pulled a waist-high fastball over the right-field fence.

The Astros handed the two-run lead back to Kazmir.

Kazmir reached the sixth inning in firm control of the game. But Lorenzo Cain sent him to the showers with a one-out double.

"To get the rally started with the double there was huge," Cain said. "Once we got him out, I feel like we were able to score a few runs."

Houston manager A.J. Hinch called upon lefty specialist Oliver Perez, who bested Hosmer in a crucial spot on Thursday. Hosmer flailed at a pair of sliders in the opposite batter's box to start their second encounter. When Perez tried a third slider, Hosmer pulled off an emergency hack, flaring an RBI single into left.

Frustrated by the Astros' defensive shifts the night before, the Royals benefited from then in the sixth. Kendrys Morales rolled a grounder toward the right of second base, where Jose Altuve no longer stood. Moustakas loaded the bases with a walk.

Oliver Perez exited the contest, but Hinch could not find a reliever capable of throwing

strikes. Josh Fields, the next man up, walked Salvador Perez on four pitches, tying the game. Perez walked only 13 times in the regular season.

"It was huge, at that point," Yost said. "Tied the ballgame up."

An inning later, Escobar led off the seventh. Magic would soon follow. Escobar noted how shallow the opposing outfielders set up. The positioning of the Astros confused him, as he explained during a postgame news conference.

"Those guys, they always play like that in the regular season, they play too shallow in the outfield," Escobar said. "Everybody is moving - second base, he's playing right behind the base. It's crazy. I don't know why those guys do that."

Seated next to him, Perez offered a coda: "Good for us," he said.

The Royals did not show panic in the aftermath of Game 1. During the proceedings of Game 2, the players demonstrated the pluck and talent that carried them to the best record in the American League. A restorative victory allowed the group a chance to exhale.

"Championship teams win those types of games right there," Hosmer said

ROYALS 5, ASTROS 4

Houston	AB	R	H	BI	BB	SO	Avg.
Altuve 2b	5	0	0	0	0	0	.300
Springer rf	3	1	1	2	1	1	.429
Correa ss	4	0	1	0	0	2	.222
Col.Rasmus lf	3	1	2	2	0	0	.500
Gattis dh	4	0	1	0	0	0	.250
Valbuena 3b	4	0	1	0	0	2	.143
Carter 1b	4	1	1	0	0	2	.250
J.Castro c	2	1	0	0	1	0	.000
a-Lowrie ph	1	0	0	0	0	1	.000
Marisnick cf	3	0	1	0	0	1	.429
b-Tucker ph	0	0	0	0	1	0	---
2-C.Gomez pr	0	0	0	0	0	0	---
Totals	33	4	8	4	4	9	
Kansas City	AB	R	H	BI	BB	SO	Avg.
A.Escobar ss	5	1	2	0	0	1	.222
Zobrist 2b	4	0	2	1	0	0	.500
L.Cain cf	4	1	1	0	0	0	.250
Hosmer 1b	4	1	1	1	0	0	.125
K.Morales dh	4	0	1	0	0	0	.375
Moustakas 3b	3	0	0	0	1	0	.000
S.Perez c	3	1	2	2	1	0	.286
A.Gordon lf	3	0	1	0	1	1	.286
1-J.Dyson pr-lf	0	0	0	0	0	0	---
Rios rf	3	1	1	0	0	1	.200
Orlando rf	1	0	0	0	0	0	.000
Totals	34	5	11	4	3	7	

Houston   121 000 000 — 4 8 0
Kansas City 011 002 10x — 5 11 0

a-struck out for J.Castro in the 9th.
b-walked for Marisnick in the 9th.
  1-ran for A.Gordon in the 8th. 2-ran for Tucker in the 9th.
  LOB: Houston 6, Kansas City 8. **2B:** Col.Rasmus (1), L.Cain (1), Rios (1). **3B:** A.Escobar (1). **HR:** Col.Rasmus (2), off Cueto; S.Perez (1), off Kazmir. **RBIs:** Springer 2 (3), Col.Rasmus 2 (4), Zobrist (1), Hosmer (1), S.Perez 2 (2).
  Runners left in scoring position: Houston 2 (Valbuena, Correa); Kansas City 4 (Rios 2, A.Escobar 2). **RISP:** Houston 3 for 6; Kansas City 3 for 8. **GIDP:** Correa, Zobrist. **DP:** Houston 1 (Valbuena, Altuve, Carter); Kansas City 1 (Moustakas, Zobrist, Hosmer).

Houston	IP	H	R	ER	BB	SO	NP	ERA
Kazmir	5⅓	5	3	3	1	4	97	5.06
O.Perez	0	2	1	1	0	0	11	27.00
J.Fields	⅓	0	0	0	1	2	13	0.00
W.Harris L, 0-1	⅓	2	1	1	0	0	9	6.75
Sipp	⅓	0	0	0	0	1	1	0.00
Neshek	⅓	2	0	0	1	1	14	0.00
Kansas City	IP	H	R	ER	BB	SO	NP	ERA
Cueto	6	7	4	3	5	10	3	6.00
K.Herrera W, 1-0	1	1	0	0	1	2	1	0.00
Madson	1	0	0	0	2	12	4	4.50
W.Davis S, 1	1	0	0	1	1	1	2	0.00

O.Perez pitched to 3 batters in the 6th.
  Blown save: J.Fields (1). **Hold:** Madson (1). **Inherited runners-scored:** O.Perez 1-1, J.Fields 3-1, Sipp 1-0.
  Umpires: Home, Angel Hernandez; First, Mike Everitt; Second, Ron Kulpa; Third, Gerry Davis; Left, Todd Tichenor; Right, Lance Barksdale. **Time:** 3:27. **Att:** 40,008.

HOW THEY SCORED

ASTROS FIRST. With one out, Springer walked. With two outs, Rasmus doubled to right, Springer scored. Astros 1, Royals 0.

ASTROS SECOND. Carter led off and singled to center. Castro walked, Carter to second. Marisnick reached on infield single to short, Carter to third, Castro to second. With one out, Springer singled to left, Carter and Castro scored, Marisnick to second. Astros 3, Royals 0.

ROYALS SECOND. With two outs, Perez homered. Astros 3, Royals 1.

ASTROS THIRD. Rasmus led off and homered to right. Astros 4, Royals 1.

ROYALS THIRD. Rios led off and doubled to center. Escobar reached on infield single to second, Rios to third. Zobrist hit into a double play, third to second to first, Rios scored. Astros 4, Royals 2.

ROYALS SIXTH. With one out, Cain doubled to right. Hosmer singled to left, Cain scored. Morales singled to center, Hosmer to third. Moustakas walked, Morales to second. Perez walked, Hosmer scored, Morales to third, Moustakas to second. Astros 4, Royals 4.

ROYALS SEVENTH. Escobar led off and tripled to right. Zobrist singled to left, Escobar scored. Royals 5, Astros 4.

DAVID EULITT

Wade Davis and Eric Hosmer (pictured) caught Astro pinch-runner Carlos Gomez napping in the ninth inning, killing a potential Houston rally.

Royals beat defensive shifts with opposite-field hits

Nine of Royals' 11 hits in ALDS Game 2 victory go to opposite field

The offense that often eluded the Royals in Game 1 of their American League Division Series was hidden behind crafty defensive shifts by the visiting Houston Astros.

"I don't think it has anything to do with analytics," Astros manager A.J. Hinch said. "I think it has everything to do with they did a pretty good job at finishing their at-bats. They're a tough team to get out."

Hinch pointed to the sixth inning in particular, when the Royals placed three consecutive hits between Astros outfielders and tied the score 4-4. The Royals had 11 hits overall - compared with six the night before - with nine of them going to the opposite field.

Eric Hosmer drove in a run in the pivotal sixth inning when he served a single to the opposite field. In the seventh, Alcides Escobar took advantage of shallow outfield positioning when he tripled to right field, and Ben Zobrist beat an infield shifted to the right side when he singled in Escobar.

"They played the shift really well, and they've been doing it all year," said Royals center fielder Lorenzo Cain. "We just have to find the holes and find a way to get on any way possible. Hopefully guys will come through in clutch situations."

"It's been working for us all year, but every once in a while you get beat with it," Astros center fielder Jake Marisnick said. "It's a little bit frustrating, but there's many times we've taken hits away doing it. There's no bad feelings about it at all."

- Kathleen Gier

Royals reliever Kelvin Herrera made some noise after he got Colby Rasmus to pop out in the seventh inning.

Ben Zobrist did a little celebrating after his single knocked in Alcides Escobar for the go-ahead run in the seventh inning.

Royals first baseman Eric Hosmer needed a moment to compose himself after fouling a ball off his leg during the third game of the American League Division Series.

JOHN SLEEZER

ALDS GAME 3

	1 2 3	4 5 6	7 8 9	R	H	E
Kansas City	0 0 0	1 0 0	0 0 1	— 2	7	0
Houston	0 0 0	0 2 1	1 0x	— 4	8	1

THE KANSAS CITY STAR

10/12/2015

Can't solve Keuchel

Astros' ace gives up just one run in seven innings as Houston wins 4-2

Down 2-1, Royals face elimination in Game 4

BY ANDY McCULLOUGH

HOUSTON

This is October: Our best versus your best, so in the seventh inning of a 4-2 loss Sunday in Game 3 of the American League Division Series, Royals All-Star Lorenzo Cain stared out 60 feet and 6 inches at Astros All-Star pitcher Dallas Keuchel. Houston manager A.J. Hinch approached the mound, but he left the ball in the hands of his ace.

"He probably knew I was going to bite his head off," Keuchel said.

As the proverbial backs of the Royals pressed against a wall, Cain represented the tying run. He had launched the lone salvo sullying Keuchel's line, a solo homer three innings before. Now the Royals required Cain to break through, to erase the pattern of failure with runners in scoring position. A runner stood on third base as Keuchel prepared to throw his 124th pitch of the day.

Keuchel rocked and fired a 90-mph fastball destined for the outer reaches of the strike zone, far from where Cain might hurt him. Cain flailed and missed. He smacked his bat with his fist. The pattern held - the best of the Royals, stars such as Eric Hosmer, Alex Gordon and Salvador Perez, could not trump Keuchel, the lodestar of Houston's rotation.

DAVID EULITT

Astros starter Dallas Keuchel showed why he was 15-0 at Minute Maid Park during the regular season, giving up just one run to the Royals in seven innings of work.

"When you get to this type of scenario and you don't capitalize, you get what happens today," Royals manager Ned Yost said. "They did."

The Royals finished the day with zero hits in seven at-bats with runners in scoring position. The Astros found two in eight chances. The difference decided the game.

After four sterling innings, Edinson Volquez stumbled in the fifth and the sixth. He coughed up a one-run lead, a thin margin to be sure, but perhaps the best expected against a stalwart southpaw like Keuchel. Astros veteran Jason Castro cracked a go-ahead, two-run single in the fifth, and outfielder Carlos Gomez ambushed Volquez for a RBI single in the sixth.

"I think I pitched pretty good tonight, especially pitching against Keuchel," Volquez said. "He's a bulldog."

Danny Duffy yielded a solo blast to Chris Carter in the seventh. Keuchel would not depart until after the seventh. He set a season-high pitch count, scattered five hits and stranded eight runners. Hosmer, Gordon and Perez combined to go zero for eight against him. Gordon walloped a leadoff homer in the ninth, but that only cut the deficit to two.

Cain led off the fourth with a 10-pitch at-bat, fouling off five in a row. He spoiled change-ups away and fastballs on the hands. At last, Keuchel hung a slider. Cain did not miss.

The blast soared over the Crawford Boxes in left field and cleared the train tracks high above the field. Cain clapped his hands, just once, as he touched home plate.

"Let's go!" he shouted as he slapped hands with Perez outside the dugout. "Let's go!"

Volquez recorded six strikeouts in the first four innings, baffling credible foes such as Jose Altuve, George Springer and Carlos Correa. Heading into the fifth, no Astro had reached second base. That changed soon after Volquez issued a one-out walk to Luis Valbuena. Up came Carter. He ripped a first-pitch fastball into the left-field corner and sprinted for a double. Valbuena held at third.

Volquez had struck out Castro with a curveball at the thighs in the third inning. Castro stared at the ball as it dipped into the strike zone. This time, Volquez shook off Perez's call for a 1-2 fastball. He tried a change-up, a pitch that "was kind of in the middle," Volquez said. Castro rolled a single back up the middle and gave Houston the lead.

The Astros padded the advantage in the next inning. Springer unloaded on the first pitch of the inning, a curveball down the middle. Cain sprinted to his right, trying to flag down the ball. He reached it with his glove, but could not hang on. Springer braked at second with a double.

"Just caught it in the palm of my glove," Cain said. "Definitely got to make that play. That's a play that I always make."

Correa advanced Springer to third. The Royals elected to intentionally walk Rasmus. After Gattis struck out, Yost allowed Volquez to face Gomez. Gomez was nursing an intercostal strain, and his swings earlier in the game looked agonizing. Yet he still lined a first-pitch single.

"It was a good pitch, down and in," Volquez said. "And he was still able to drive the ball to center field. There's nothing you can do about it."

The ball landed near Cain's feet. He was hamstrung by the ball's flight, unable to charge for a dive, unable to stop Houston's

relentless rush. As the decibel level skyrocketed once more, the best of the Royals could not stop the best of the Astros.

Alex Rios led off the seventh with a walk. Escobar chased a 3-2 pitch for a ground-out, which at least advanced Rios. Ben Zobrist tried to sneak a bunt single, but could not push the ball far enough down the third-base line. So it was up to Cain, whose arrival prompted Hinch to visit the mound.

"I figured he was going to let me pitch to their best hitter, and I thought I deserved it," Keuchel said.

Cain fouled off a 2-0 change-up and missed another one. He took another change-up. But with the count full, he chased a sinker outside his reach.

"I think it was a ball," Cain said. "Little too aggressive there. That's what he (Keuchel) does."

Gordon provided a lift with his solo shot against closer Luke Gregerson in the ninth. Escobar singled, bringing the tying run to the plate. But Zobrist hit into a fielder's choice and Cain struck out, ending it.

"We've got to win two, they've got to win one," Yost said. "But we come out (today) and we win, then it's excitement back at The K for Game 5. So we're looking forward to that."

ASTROS 4, ROYALS 2

Kansas City	AB	R	H	BI	BB	SO	Avg.
A.Escobar ss	5	0	2	0	0	0	.286
Zobrist 2b	4	0	1	0	0	1	.417
L.Cain cf	4	1	1	1	1	2	.250
Hosmer 1b	4	0	0	0	0	3	.083
K.Morales dh	3	0	1	0	1	0	.364
Moustakas 3b	4	0	1	0	0	1	.100
S.Perez c	3	0	0	0	1	1	.200
A.Gordon lf	4	1	1	1	0	2	.273
Rios rf	3	0	0	0	1	0	.125
Totals	34	2	7	2	4	10	

Houston	AB	R	H	BI	BB	SO	Avg.
Altuve 2b	4	0	0	0	0	1	.214
Springer rf	4	1	1	0	0	2	.364
Correa ss	4	0	1	0	0	1	.231
Col.Rasmus lf	1	0	1	0	3	0	.571
Gattis dh	4	0	0	0	0	2	.167
C.Gomez cf	4	0	1	1	0	2	.250
Valbuena 3b	1	1	0	0	1	1	.125
a-Ma.Gonzalez ph-3b	1	0	0	0	0	0	.000
b-Lowrie ph-3b	1	0	0	0	0	0	.000
Carter 1b	3	2	3	1	0	0	.455
J.Castro c	3	0	1	2	0	1	.111
Totals	30	4	8	4	4	10	

Kansas City	000	100	001	—	2	7	0
Houston	000	021	10x	—	4	8	1

a-popped out for Valbuena in the 6th.
b-flied out for Ma.Gonzalez in the 8th.
E: Valbuena (1). **LOB:** Kansas City 10, Houston 6. **2B:** Zobrist (1), Moustakas (1), Springer (1), Carter (1). **HR:** L.Cain (1), off Keuchel; A.Gordon (1), off Gregerson; Carter (1), off D.Duffy. **RBIs:** L.Cain (1), A.Gordon (1), C.Gomez (1), Carter (1), J.Castro 2 (2). **S:** Zobrist.
Runners left in scoring position: Kansas City 5 (Hosmer 2, A.Gordon 2, L.Cain); Houston 2 (Ma.Gonzalez, Lowrie). **RISP:** Kansas City 0 for 7; Houston 2 for 8.
Runners moved up: A.Escobar, L.Cain, Moustakas, S.Perez, Correa. **GIDP:** Altuve.
DP: Kansas City 1 (A.Escobar, Zobrist, Hosmer).

Kansas City	IP	H	R	ER	BB	SO	NP	ERA
Volquez L, 0-1	5⅓	5	3	4	8	87		4.76
D.Duffy	⅔	1	1	0	0	6	13.50	
Hochevar	1⅓	2	0	0	2	22	0.00	

Houston	IP	H	R	ER	BB	SO	NP	ERA
Keuchel W, 1-0	7	5	1	3	7	124	1.29	
Sipp	⅔	0	0	1	2	18	0.00	
Gregerson S, 2	1⅓	2	1	0	1	16	3.86	

Holds: Sipp (2). **Inherited runners-scored:** D.Duffy 2-0, Gregerson 1-0. **IBB:** off Volquez (Col.Rasmus), off Keuchel (L.Cain). **WP:** Keuchel.
Umpires: Home, Mike Everitt; First, Ron Kulpa; Second, Gerry Davis; Third, Todd Tichenor; Left, Lance Barksdale; Right, Angel Hernandez. **Time:** 3:20. **Att:** 42,674.

HOW THEY SCORED

ROYALS FOURTH: Cain led off and homered to left. Royals 1, Astros 0.

ASTROS FIFTH: With one out, Valbuena walked. Carter doubled to left, Valbuena to third. Castro singled to center, Valbuena and Carter scored. Astros 2, Royals 1.

ASTROS SIXTH: Springer led off and doubled to center. Correa grounded out to second, Springer to third. Rasmus was intentionally walked. With two outs, Gomez singled to center, Springer scored, Rasmus to second. Astros 3, Royals 1.

ASTROS SEVENTH: Carter led off and homered to left. Astros 4, Royals 1.

ROYALS NINTH: Gordon led off and homered to left. Astros 4, Royals 2.

JOHN SLEEZER

Royals starter Edinson Volquez walked to the dugout after being relieved in the sixth. Volquez started out strong but faded in the fifth and sixth innings.

A day of frustration

During the season, the Royals hit .269 as a team, a healthy percentage that ranked second in baseball.

But in pressure situations they were even better.

With two outs and runners in scoring position, the team batting average jumped to .277, some 34 points higher than the American League average. Three Royals - Lorenzo Cain, Kendrys Morales and Eric Hosmer - ranked among the top eight in that category.

That skill failed the Royals on Sunday in their 4-2 loss to the Astros in Game 3 of the American League Division Series.

On a day in which the approach to Astros starter Dallas Keuchel was superb at times by showing patience when required and jumping on pitches when he made a mistake, the Royals could not finish innings that started with promise.

They went zero for seven with runners in scoring position.

"At times with runners in scoring position we probably swung as some balls that probably wouldn't have been called strikes," Royals manager Ned Yost said.

"He has good movement and that's what good movement does," Yost said. "He moves location in and out, changes speeds. I think he should be the Cy Young winner this year."

- Blair Kerkhoff

Royals' third baseman Mike Moustakas lept in vain for a double hit by Astros first baseman Chris Carter in the fifth inning.

Astros second baseman Jose Altuve nearly turned a double play over Royals shortstop Alcides Escobar in the ninth.

Kansas City Royals' Lorenzo Cain follows through on an RBI single to score Alex Rios in front of Houston Astros catcher Jason Castro.

JOHN SLEEZER

ALDS GAME 4

	123	456	789	R	H	E
Kansas City	020	000	052	9	8	0
Houston	011	010	300	6	9	1

     L W L W 5

THE KANSAS CITY STAR

10/13/2015

Back from the brink

....

Royals win 9-6 after trailing Astros by four runs after seven innings

....

KC scores five in the eighth inning and sends series to deciding Game 5

....

———————

BY ANDY McCULLOUGH

HOUSTON

Ned Yost gazed at his feet as he traversed the bowels of Minute Maid Park, exiting a Royals clubhouse still humming after a comeback that kept a season alive and stunned even the heartiest of the faithful.

The hallways were quiet as Yost strode toward his postgame news conference. Along the way, he walked by the hushed confines of the Houston Astros, who saw their champagne celebration canceled by a 9-6 victory by the Royals in Game 4. Yost could believe it - he had seen something so similar in last year's Wild Card Game - and yet he could not.

"That kind of came out of nowhere, huh?" Yost said. He shook his head, still trying to process the result. "Sometimes there's things that are meant to be."

Stop us if you've heard this one before: Down four runs in the eighth, six outs away from an early winter, the Royals stormed back to astonish their opponents. It sounds improbable only because it sounds so familiar. The debate will rage about which comeback was better: The extra-inning scramble to defeat Oakland last year or the five-run ambush to wreck a coronation in Houston?

The victory over the Athletics opened the door to a franchise-restoring run to the World Series. The story of the 2015 Royals remains unfinished, but they earned the chance to write at least one more chapter.

"The percentages of baseball certainly weren't in our favor," general manager Dayton Moore said. "These guys went out and took the game."

For seven innings, the Royals looked lifeless. In the eighth, they became the undead, refusing to let their season perish. An innocuous single by Alex Rios soon mushroomed into a bases-loaded situation with none out for Lorenzo Cain. He roped a single. Eric Hosmer smacked only his second hit in 16 postseason at-bats to cut the deficit to two.

A swing by Kendrys Morales and an error by rookie shortstop Carlos Correa tied the game. Morales punched a grounder up the middle. The ball evaded reliever Tony Sipp and caromed off the mound. Correa rushed forward and felt the ball bounce off his glove. Cain raced home to tie the game and set up Alex Gordon's eventual RBI.

"We love each other," Gordon said. "We have fun together. And we fight together. That's what we did today. We never gave up."

The top of the inning lasted 40 minutes. The bottom lasted seven pitches. Wade Davis threw all of them. He also handled the ninth for the two-inning save.

The Royals claimed the lead in the second inning. Salvador Perez clobbered an opposite-field shot for a two-run homer.

The Astros tied the game with two solo blasts. Yordano Ventura, on the mound only three days after his last start, hung a curveball in the bottom of the second, and Carlos Gomez deposited it into the Crawford Boxes in left. An inning later, Correa pulled his hands inside and hammered a 96-mph fastball. The pitch was a ball, and still Correa powered it out.

Alex Gordon (right) welcomed home Eric Hosmer, who scored on Gordon's ground-out during Kansas City's furious rally.

JOHN SLEEZER

Correa bested Ventura once more in the fifth. Ventura issued a two-out walk to outfielder George Springer. With the count full, Ventura hummed a fastball over the heart of the plate. Correa ripped a rocket into right. The ball evaded Hosmer's glove by inches and rattled off the wall. Springer's helmet flew off his head as he barreled home for the go-ahead run.

When Lance McCullers hit Perez in the seventh, Yost fired his fastest bullet. Terrance Gore replaced Perez at first base. He

Anatomy of a Royal rally How the Royals flipped the script to erase a four-run deficit in the eighth inning:

S7	S8	S8	S7	S9	E6	K	BB	4-2	BB	ꓘ
Rios singles to left	Escobar singles to center	Zobrist singles to center	Cain singles; Rios scores, 6-3 Astros	Hosmer singles; Escobar scores, 6-4 Astros	Morales safe on error; Zobrist, Cain score, tied 6-6	Moustakas strikes out	Butera walks	Gordon grounds out; Hosmer scores, 7-6 KC	Rios walks	Escobar strikes out

JOHN SLEEZER

Frowns turned upside down as Mike Moustakas (center) welcomed home Ben Zobrist and Lorenzo Cain after they scored during the Royals' eighth-inning rally.

stole second on the first pitch from reliever Will Harris. There he idled while Gordon struck out. But with Rios at the plate, Gore jetted into third.

Both of his feet arrived before Luis Valbuena dropped a tag. The momentum from Gore spilled Valbuena into foul territory. Houston manager A.J. Hinch challenged the call. The replay showed that Gore's feet left the bag for a split second; it was unclear if Valbuena kept his glove on during the interlude.

The replay crew in New York ruled Gore out, a decision that stunned the Royals. Yet the two homers against Ryan Madson, for whatever reason, appeared to have the opposite effect.

When the inning ended, Mike Moustakas charged off the diamond and lit up the dugout with expletives.

"I'm not ready to go home yet!" he hollered.

The message acted like kindling. Just as it did in the eighth inning against Oakland, the dugout came alive.

Up came Rios, who had only one hit in the series entering Monday's eighth inning. He roped a first-pitch cutter off Harris for a single. Alcides Escobar shuttled a curveball up the middle for another hit. Ben Zobrist deposited a hanging curveball into center for a third single.

"We had our biggest at-bats at the most important times," Moore said.

Astros Manager A. J. Hinch stuck with Harris to face Cain. He roped a single into left to bring home a run. Now Hosmer entered the fray, aware of his miserable postseason, hoping to alter the narrative with one swing. But he did not aim for the fences.

Hosmer fouled back two fastballs from Sipp, a southpaw. He ignored two sliders in the dirt. Then he ripped an RBI single into right, opening the door for Morales' grounder and Correa's error.

With the game tied, Sipp struck out Moustakas. Hinch sent Luke Gregerson to face backup catcher Drew Butera. It was Butera's first postseason plate appearance, and he walked.

The bases were loaded for Gordon. He was hitless for the day, with little success all series. He found a heater and bounced it into second baseman Jose Altuve's glove.

"I was pumping my fist after getting an out," Gordon said. "I usually don't do that."

A thrilled group of teammates greeted both Gordon and Hosmer after the run. Hosmer would later crush a homer off reliever Josh Fields in the ninth. Wade Davis smothered the Astros for the last sixth outs. One man accomplished what four Astros could not.

On the ground floor of Minute Maid Park, walking toward his news conference, Yost kept shaking his head. He had watched his team to do this before. To see it again was a welcome sight.

"They just don't quit," Yost said. "They just don't quit."

ROYALS 9, ASTROS 6

Kansas City	AB	R	H	BI	BB	SO	Avg.
Escobar ss	4	1	1	0	0	2	.278
Zobrist 2b	4	2	1	0	1	0	.375
Cain cf	5	1	1	1	0	3	.235
Hosmer 1b	5	2	2	3	0	1	.176
Morales dh	4	0	0	1	0	1	.267
3-Dyson pr-dh	1	0	0	0	0	1	.000
Moustakas 3b	4	1	1	0	1	1	.143
Perez c	2	1	1	2	0	0	.250
1-Gore pr	0	0	0	0	0	0	–
Butera c	0	0	0	0	1	0	–
Gordon lf	3	0	0	1	1	1	.214
Rios rf	3	1	1	0	1	2	.182
4-Orlando pr-rf	0	0	0	0	0	0	.000
Totals	**35**	**9**	**8**	**8**	**5**	**12**	

Houston	AB	R	H	BI	BB	SO	Avg.
Altuve 2b	4	1	0	0	1	1	.167
Springer rf	4	1	0	0	1	4	.267
Correa ss	4	2	4	4	0	0	.412
Col.Rasmus lf	4	1	2	1	1	2	.545
Gattis dh	4	0	1	0	0	1	.188
2-Marisnick pr-dh	0	0	0	0	0	0	.429
b-Tucker ph	1	0	0	0	0	1	.000
C.Gomez cf	5	1	2	1	0	1	.333
Valbuena 3b	2	0	0	0	2	0	.100
Carter 1b	3	0	0	0	0	2	.357
Ma.Gonzalez 1b	1	0	0	0	0	1	.000
J.Castro c	3	0	0	0	0	3	.083
a-Lowrie ph	1	0	0	0	0	0	.000
Conger c	0	0	0	0	0	0	–
Totals	**36**	**6**	**9**	**6**	**5**	**16**	

Kansas City	**020**	**000**	**052**	**–**	**9**	**8**	**0**
Houston	**011**	**010**	**300**	**–**	**6**	**9**	**1**

a-popped out for J.Castro in the 8th. 1-ran for Perez in the 7th. 2-ran for Gattis in the 7th. 3-ran for Morales in the 8th. 4-ran for Rios in the 8th.

E: Correa (1). **LOB:** Kansas City 6, Houston 9. **2B:** Correa (1). **HR:** Perez (2), off McCullers; Hosmer (1), off J.Fields; C.Gomez (1), off Ventura; Correa (1), off Ventura; Correa (2), off Madson; Col.Rasmus (3), off Madson. **RBIs:** Cain (2), Hosmer 3 (4), Morales (3), Perez 2 (4), Gordon (2), Correa 4 (4), Col.Rasmus (5), C.Gomez (2). **SB:** Dyson (2), Gore (1). **CS:** Gore (1).

Runners left in scoring position: Kansas City 2 (Escobar 2); Houston 4 (Gattis 2, Ma.Gonzalez 2). **RISP:** Kansas City 3 for 8; Houston 0 for 4. **Runners moved up:** Gordon.

Kansas City	IP	H	R	ER	BB	SO	NP	ERA
Ventura	5	4	3	3	3	8	93	7.71
Herrera	1	0	1	1	2	3	26	3.00
Madson W, 1-0	1	4	2	2	0	2	23	9.00
Davis S, 2	2	1	0	0	0	3	24	0.00

Houston	IP	H	R	ER	BB	SO	NP	ERA
McCullers	6⅓	2	2	2	2	7	110	2.84
W.Harris	⅔	4	4	3	0	1	18	18.00
Sipp L, 0-1	⅓	1	1	0	0	1	17	0.00
Gregerson	⅔	0	0	0	2	1	24	3.00
J.Fields	1	1	2	2	1	2	19	10.80

W.Harris pitched to 4 batters in the 8th. K.Herrera pitched to 1 batter in the 7th.

Hold: W.Harris (2). **Blown save:** Sipp (1). **Inherited runners-scored:** Madson 1-1, W.Harris 1-0, Sipp 3-3, Gregerson 2-1. **IBB:** off Ventura (Col.Rasmus). **HBP:** by Ventura (Correa), by McCullers (A.Escobar, S.Perez).

Umpires: Home, Ron Kulpa; First, Gerry Davis; Second, Todd Tichenor; Third, Lance Barksdale; Left, Angel Hernandez; Right, Mike Everitt. **Time:** 4:05. **Att:** 42,387.

HOW THEY SCORED

ROYALS SECOND: With one out, Moustakas walked. Perez homered to right. Royals 2, Astros 0.
ASTROS SECOND: Gomez led off and homered to left. Royals 2, Astros 1.
ASTROS THIRD: With two outs, Correa homered to left. Royals 2, Astros 2.
ASTROS FIFTH: With two outs, Springer walked. Correa doubled to right, Springer scored. Astros 3, Royals 2.
ASTROS SEVENTH: Altuve led off and walked. With one out, Correa homered to left, Altuve scored. Rasmus homered to right. Astros 6, Royals 2.
ROYALS EIGHTH: Rios led off and singled to left. Escobar singled to center, Rios to second. Zobrist singled to center, Rios to third, Escobar to second. Cain singled to left, Rios scored, Escobar to third, Zobrist to second. Hosmer singled to right, Escobar scored, Zobrist to third, Cain to second. Morales safe on fielder's choice and Correa's error, Zobrist and L.Cain scored, Hosmer to third. Dyson pinch ran for Morales. Dyson stole second. With one out, Butera walked. Gordon grounded out to second, Hosmer scored, Dyson to third, Butera to second. Royals 7, Astros 6.
ROYALS NINTH: Zobrist led off and walked. With one out, Hosmer homered to center, Zobrist scored. Royals 9, Astros 6.

Davis goes long

After recording a three-out save in the Royals' Game 2 victory, Wade Davis was called into Monday's game once the Royals took a 7-6 lead into the bottom of the eighth inning.

Royals manager Ned Yost had said he would use any of his top relievers - Kelvin Herrera, Ryan Madson or Davis - in a two-inning appearance Monday. Only Davis was called on for the extra duty, and he retired six of the seven hitters he faced.

"Having Wade come out and get a six-out save gave us the best opportunity to win the game," Yost said. "And that's exactly what we meant to do."

Davis' cushion increased in the ninth after Eric Hosmer's two-run homer in the top half of the inning, but his approach didn't despite the longer outing.

"You just go out there and try to make good pitches and let your defense handle business," Davis said.

Monday marked Davis' third postseason two-inning appearance. It happened twice last year, and he became the third player to notch a two-inning save for the Royals in the playoffs, joining Steve Mingori (Game 4, 1976 ALCS) and Dan Quisenberry (Game 4, 1980 World Series).

- Chris Fickett and Blair Kerkhoff

Royals' third baseman Mike Moustakas fields a ball hit by Houston Astros second baseman Jose Altuve in the fifth inning.

A replay determined that Terrance Gore was out after his foot came off third base and Houston's Luis Valbuena tagged him during an attempted steal in the seventh inning.

The Royals and starting pitcher Johnny Cueto (foreground) celebrated after their 7-2 win over the Houston Astros on Wednesday night sent Kansas City to the American League Championship Series for the second straight year.

DAVID EULITT

ALDS GAME 5

	1 2 3	4 5 6	7 8 9		R	H	E
Houston	020	000	000	—	2	2	0
Kansas City	000	130	03x	—	7	8	0

THE KANSAS CITY STAR

10/15/2015

KC takes the fifth

Royals win series 3-2 and advance to play Blue Jays in ALCS

Johnny Cueto pitches eight strong innings

BY ANDY McCULLOUGH

Johnny Cueto shook both his fists as he strutted off the diamond, as if absorbing the electricity pulsing through Kauffman Stadium, a ballpark galvanized by the finest outing of Cueto's brief Royals career.

Cueto's dreadlocks shook as he completed the seventh inning. He saved his best for the biggest night, a 7-2 victory in Game 5 to wrest the American League Division Series from the upstart Astros.

Two years ago, Cueto heard his name spat out in derision as a visiting player during a playoff game in Pittsburgh. During Wednesday's eighth inning, his name rang out across a sold-out ballpark, each syllable coated with a love and trust earned on this night.

Maligned for so much of his Kansas City tenure, Cueto strapped the rest of the Royals to his back across eight innings. He attacked Houston batters with his fastball, baffled them with his change-up and delivered on the promise elicited by his arrival in late July. He retired the last 19 batters he faced.

"Johnny was phenomenal. He's an ace," Royals second baseman Ben Zobrist said. "He struggled a little bit toward the end of the season, but he proved tonight that he is as advertised. He is that guy that they thought he was coming over in the trade."

Wade Davis pitched a perfect ninth for the Royals.

Cueto lamented one misplaced pitch, a fastball vaporized by third baseman Luis Valbuena for a two-run homer in the second. Cueto struck out eight as the Royals advanced to the American League Championship Series for the second season in a row. They will play host to Toronto in Game 1 at 7:07 p.m. Friday night.

Granted new life by a frenetic comeback in Game 4, the Royals outlasted the Astros across five harrowing games. Houston operated in the driver's seat for much of these five days and nights. Yet Kansas City displayed enough mettle, and enough timely hitting, to extend its season.

As Cueto glimmered on the mound, his teammates punched through the decaying foundation of the Astros' pitching staff. Alex Rios smacked a two-run double and came around to score during a go-ahead, three-run rally in the fifth. The defense shined through the evening: Zobrist leaped and snagged to snag a liner at second base, and Alex Gordon slid on his back and caught a ball in foul territory.

In the eighth, Kendrys Morales vanquished Houston's ace, Dallas Keuchel, who appeared in relief. Morales boomed a three-run homer. He spread his arms wide as he rounded first base. The dugout and the ballpark erupted as one. Morales rolled his shoulders and slapped his fingers across his neck when he reached the plate, repeating the gesture from Astros pitcher Lance McCullers that infuriated the Royals in Game 4.

TAMMY LJUNGBLAD

Royals right fielder Alex Rios had the key hit in Wednesday's victory over the Astros, a two-run double in the fifth inning at Kauffman Stadium.

Hours before the game, Ned Yost settled into his seat for a news conference and strummed his fingers against the microphone. His answers were clipped at the start. His bullpen was fully loaded. His leash with Cueto would depend on Cueto's performance. Yost kept his enthusiasm restrained, but it was apparent.

"It's going to be a fun game," Yost said. "Going to be a fun night."

Kauffman Stadium pulsated after a stirring pregame tribute to Larry Leggio and John Mesh, the two Kansas City firefighters killed during a building collapse on Monday. Cueto followed up with a scoreless, three-batter inning in the top of the first.

The noise dipped in the second. Evan Gattis pulled a fastball down the third-base line. Mike Moustakas gloved it, but his momentum carried him over the line. His throw to first pulled Eric Hosmer off the bag. Hosmer swung his glove to tag Gattis, only to lose control of the ball.

The two-out single proved costly. On the next pitch, Valbuena hammered a 94-mph fastball into the Astros bullpen.

Collin McHugh was Cueto's counterpart on the mound. In Game 1, he limited the Royals to two runs and four hits in six innings. He began Game 5 in much the same fashion. McHugh does not possess starling velocity or one vicious off-speed pitch. He relies upon upsetting the timing of his opponents.

The Royals played into this trap at the start. The Astros turned two double plays in the first three innings. Kansas City required some good fortune to score its first run.

With one out in the fourth, Lorenzo Cain hacked at a low fastball and smacked a cue shot into right field. His teammates ribbed him as he ran down the line. Cain broke for second on a full-count cutter, which Hosmer dumped into center for a single. Carlos Gomez lost his footing as he retrieved the baseball, and Cain sprinted all the way home.

Cueto recovered from his second blip to author one of his finest outings as a Royal. He struck out seven through five innings. After Valbuena's homer, Cueto settled into a rhythm.

McHugh survived flurries of hard contact until

the fifth. He hit Salvador Perez with a full-count curveball. Gordon one-hopped a ground-rule double on a pitiable, belt-high cutter. Astros manager A.J. Hinch fetched McHugh and inserted Mike Fiers, a starter who had not pitched since Sept. 29.

The decision backfired. Rios punched a curveball down the third-base line. The ball skipped over the bag and eluded Valbuena's glove. The ballpark came unglued as Perez and Gordon reached home. At second base, Rios unfurled a tremendous fist pump, his most public show of emotion as a Royal.

Alcides Escobar bunted Rios over to third base. Zobrist brought him home with a fly ball to right. A mass of Royals greeted Rios as he reached the dugout. More raucous celebrations would soon follow.

"That's a great feeling right there," Hosmer said. "We know late in the game, if we can just get a lead and hand it off to the bullpen, it's a good feeling for us. All we needed was Wader down there, and Johnny Cueto did the job for us."

ROYALS 7, ASTROS 2

Houston	AB	R	H	BI	BB	SO	Avg.
Altuve 2b	4	0	0	0	0	0	.136
Springer rf	4	0	0	0	0	2	.211
Correa ss	3	0	0	0	0	0	.350
Col.Rasmus lf	3	0	0	0	0	3	.429
C.Gomez cf	3	0	0	0	0	1	.250
Gattis dh	3	1	1	0	0	1	.211
Valbuena 3b	3	1	1	2	0	0	.154
Carter 1b	3	0	0	0	0	1	.294
J.Castro c	2	0	0	0	0	0	.071
a-Tucker ph	1	0	0	0	0	1	.000
Totals	29	2	2	0	0	9	

Kansas City	AB	R	H	BI	BB	SO	Avg.
A.Escobar ss	3	1	1	0	0	0	.286
Zobrist 2b	2	0	0	1	1	1	.333
L.Cain cf	3	2	1	0	1	0	.250
Hosmer 1b	4	0	1	1	0	0	.190
K.Morales dh	4	1	1	3	0	0	.263
Moustakas 3b	4	0	0	0	0	0	.111
S.Perez c	2	1	1	0	0	0	.286
A.Gordon lf	3	1	1	0	0	1	.235
Rios rf	3	1	2	2	0	1	.286
Orlando rf	0	0	0	0	0	0	.000
Totals	28	7	8	7	2	3	

Houston	020	000	000 —	2 2 0
Kansas City	000	130	03x —	7 8 0

a-struck out for J.Castro in the 9th.
   LOB: Houston 0, Kansas City 2. **2B:** A.Escobar (1), A.Gordon (1), Rios (2). **HR:** Valbuena (1), off Cueto; K.Morales (3), off Keuchel. **RBIs:** Valbuena 2 (2), Zobrist (2), Hosmer (5), K.Morales 3 (6), Rios 2 (2). **S:** A.Escobar. **SF:** Zobrist.
   RISP: Houston 0 for 0; Kansas City 2 for 4. **GIDP:** L.Cain, A.Gordon. **DP:** Houston 2 (Valbuena, Altuve, Carter), (Valbuena, Correa, Carter).

Houston	IP	H	R	ER	BB	SO	NP	ERA
McHugh L, 1-1	4	5	3	3	1	1	72	4.50
Fiers	1	1	1	1	0	0	9	9.00
Sipp	1⅓	0	0	0	0	1	17	0.00
Neshek	⅓	0	0	0	0	1	6	0.00
Keuchel	1	2	3	3	1	0	27	4.50

Kansas City	IP	H	R	ER	BB	SO	NP	ERA
Cueto W, 1-0	8	2	2	2	0	8	91	3.86
W.Davis	1	0	0	0	0	1	8	0.00

McHugh pitched to 2 batters in the 5th.
   Inherited runners-scored: Fiers 2-2.
IBB: off Keuchel (L.Cain). **HBP:** by McHugh (S.Perez).
   Umpires: Home, Gerry Davis; First, Todd Tichenor; Second, Lance Barksdale; Third, Angel Hernandez; Left, Mike Everitt; Right, Ron Kulpa. **Time:** 2:42. **Att:** 40,566.

HOW THEY SCORED

ASTROS SECOND: Rasmus struck out. C.Gomez flied out to left fielder Gordon. Gattis infield single to third. Valbuena home-red to right on a 0-0 count, Gattis scored. Carter fouled out to right fielder Rios. Astros 2, Royals 0.
ROYALS FOURTH: Zobrist struck out. Cain singled to right. Hosmer singled to center, Cain scored. Morales fouled out to second baseman Altuve. Mous-takas popped out to left fielder Rasmus. Astros 2, Royals 1.
ROYALS FIFTH: Perez was hit by a pitch. Gordon doubled to right, Perez to third. Fiers pitch-ing. Rios doubled to left, Perez scored, Gordon scored. Escobar sacrificed, third baseman Val-buena to sec-ond baseman Altuve, Rios to third. Zobrist hit a sacrifice fly to right fielder Springer, Rios scored. Cain grounded out, second baseman Altuve to first baseman Carter. Royals 4, Astros 2.
ROYALS EIGHTH: Keuchel pitch-ing. A.Escobar doubled to right. Zobrist lined out to sec-ond base-man Altuve. Cain was intentionally walked. Hosmer fouled out to catcher Castro. Morales homered to center on a 2-2 count, Escobar scored, Cain scored. Moustakas grounded out, shortstop Correa to first baseman Carter. Royals 7, Astros 2.

DAVID EULITT

Royals designated hitter Kendrys Morales added insurance runs with a three-run homer in the eighth inning during Wednesday's ALDS Game 5 at Kauffman Stadium.

Cain cuts a dashing figure for first run

He goes from first to home in 10.5 seconds

It took center fielder Lorenzo Cain just 10.5 seconds to cross home plate and breathe life back into the Royals during Game 5 of the American League Division Series.

With the Royals trailing by two runs, Cain started the play on first base and took off as soon as Eric Hosmer's bat struck the ball. The bloop single landed in shallow center field in front of the Astros' Carlos Gomez, who slid to his seat as the ball arrived.

Cain kept wheeling and scored the crucial first run of the Royals' 7-2 victory against the Houston Astros. It was his fourth run of the postseason, and he topped out at 20.3 mph according to Statcast.

For fans who followed Cain when he was the ALCS MVP in 2014, his speed is nothing new.

Cain reached a top speed of 20.5 mph to score from second on a Hosmer single in the first inning of Game 2. Then, he reached third on a single from Hosmer in the third, accelerating to 19.7 mph. He tapped into his speed again in the fifth inning for a stolen base at 20.4 mph.

- Kathleen Gier

TAMMY LJUNGBLAD

JOHN SLEEZER

On his way to a Game 5 victory, Johnny Cueto struck out eight and retired 19 batters in a row.

JOHN SLEEZER

Royals center fielder Lorenzo Cain (left), shortstop Alcides Escobar (center) and designated hitter Kendrys Morales celebrated on the field after defeating the Houston Astros.

Royals are taking all of their fans on another magical postseason ride

THE EDITORIAL BOARD

A 2015 baseball season so full of promise was crashing to a disheartening end, and many blue-to-the-core fans were resigned to that fact. Even the germ of this editorial began with that fate in mind on Monday afternoon. And yet ...

After being left for dead when they trailed the Houston Astros late in that day's game at Minute Maid Park, the resurgent Kansas City Royals will host the American League Championship Series starting tonight at Kauffman Stadium.

Improbable? Absolutely.

Impossible? Not for these Royals.

Behind the lights-out pitching of Johnny Cueto and the timely hitting of Alex Gordon, Alex Rios and Kendrys Morales, the team defeated the Astros 7-2 Wednesday night before a raucous, sold-out crowd at Kauffman to win the American League Division Series three games to two.

That enthralling victory came just a couple of days after the Royals shocked the Astros - and the baseball gods - by scoring seven runs in the eighth and ninth innings to win the fourth game in Houston.

After taking the division series, the Royals celebrated with their fans late into Wednesday night, well aware that the next challenge on the field likely will be even tougher.

The hard-hitting Toronto Blue Jays will swagger into Kansas City fresh off their own comeback - a three-game sweep of the Texas Rangers after losing the first two contests at home.

Throughout the Kansas City area, hundreds of thousands of Royals fans are enjoying a postseason ride they hope won't end until the team wins the World Series a few weeks from now.

This is also the perfect time to celebrate how baseball is bringing this region together again, just as it did in 2014.

At least as long as this magical run continues, forget Kansas vs. Missouri. And Kansas City vs. the suburbs. And the Jayhawks vs. the Tigers. This is one metropolitan area right now, with one common team for sports fans to root for in their daily lives.

It's also tempting to contemplate how these Royals represent the never-say-die spirit of many people in this community.

Many fans will see themselves in the Royals, as they battle different kinds of odds every day - a health problem, trouble at work, a family crisis - and try to persevere through them.

Of course, we've been here before. Just last year, in fact.

The surprising 2014 postseason run began with a wild wild-card victory, three straight more wins in the division series, followed by a four-game sweep in the league championships and the eventual seventh-game loss in the World Series to the San Francisco Giants.

How could 2015 compare with that?

Actually, it's stacking up pretty well so far. The Royals trailed by two runs or more in all five games against the Astros, yet still won three of them.

The Royals - in that fantastic comeback game on Monday - overcame a late four-run deficit just as they had last year in the wild-card victory against the Oakland Athletics.

The 2015 season is becoming extra special for one more

THROUGHOUT THE KANSAS CITY METROPOLITAN AREA, ROYALS FANS ARE ENJOYING A BASEBALL HIGH THEY HOPE WON'T END UNTIL THE CLUB WINS THE WORLD SERIES A FEW WEEKS FROM NOW.

reason: Too many people didn't expect it.

Oh, we're not talking about Royals fans. But as Eric Hosmer wrote for The Players' Tribune in a recent piece titled "No Fluke," the club's players saw many doubters around the nation before the year started.

"For us, we feel like we aren't just playing for this year," he wrote. "We're playing for last year as well. We're playing to win the pennant. But we're also playing to prove that last year's pennant was real. We're playing to prove that the 'heartbreaking ending' to our season was only one of those things. That yeah, it was heartbreaking. But it wasn't an ending at all."

When the Royals opened the season last April with a 10-1 thumping of the Chicago White Sox, it gave the city a sense that, yes, this team was real.

The Royals spent the rest of the year in first place in their division. They played through pain. They survived several key injuries. They survived the chicken pox. They defied all the professional, and not so professional, naysayers who had no

respect for the blue crew from a small-market town in the heart of America.

The team went on to fill the stands night after night through 81 home games. The team went on to lead the league in a variety of ways. The team went on to mint some unlikely and very welcome heroes. They included Morales and Ben Zobrist, along with the unshakeable Wade Davis and the surprising Brazilian speedster Paulo Orlando. The quiet overlord of this realm of young and talented ball players remained Ned Yost.

Then came Monday's thrilling, season-extending climax, just as it seemed the Royals would be eliminated by the young, talented Houstonites.

After the Royals won the final game of the division series, it meant that the club will play in even more meaningful postseason games in coming days. Just as Hosmer and his teammates wanted. And just as Royals fans always believed would happen.

Right?

Starting pitcher Edinson Volquez was fired up as he walked off the field after getting out of a jam in the sixth inning of Game 1 of the ALCS.

JOHN SLEEZER

ALCS GAME 1

	123	456	789	R	H	E
Toronto	000	000	000	0	3	1
Kansas City	002	100	02x	5	8	1

 (W) (2) (3) (4) (5) (6) (7)

THE KANSAS CITY STAR

10/17/2015

No noise from Jays

Edinson Volquez silences Toronto bats in 5-0 win in first game of ALCS

He escapes sixth inning without any damage and turns it over to pen

Salvador Perez hits a home run in the fourth

BY ANDY McCULLOUGH

Life on a tightrope must exhaust a man, so Edinson Volquez slowed his gait as he walked off the mound Friday night. He had just thrown 111 pitches, 37 of them in the sixth inning of a 5-0 Royals victory in Game 1 of the American League Championship Series. The crowd at Kauffman Stadium had chanted his name and would so do so again, and Volquez pointed to the masses and thumped his heart before he disappeared into the dugout.

Behind him, Toronto stars Josh Donaldson and Jose Bautista trudged to their dugout. Volquez had walked both men starting the torturous sixth. After that, neither man advanced a step, watching as Volquez sneaked through the inning.

A different Royal rewarded manager Ned Yost for the same strategy two innings later. Yost sent Ryan Madson, who absorbed tremendous damage from the Blue Jays on multiple occasions in the regular season, to pitch the eighth after a dynamic, brief seventh inning from Kelvin Herrera. Madson gave up a single to Donaldson and walked Bautista but still escaped with a scoreless inning.

What guided Yost during those moments of crisis? Perhaps it was faith in his players, perhaps it was a belief in their fortitude. Perhaps it was inertia, the resistance to break from routine this early in a series.

JOHN SLEEZER

Royals first baseman Eric Hosmer celebrated on second base behind Toronto Blue Jays shortstop Troy Tulowitzki after doubling to score Alcides Escobar in the eighth inning.

Volquez provided six scoreless innings, gave up two hits, walked four and struck out five. He expended himself in the process.

Alcides Escobar doubled in a run in the third and scored soon after. Salvador Perez popped his third homer of the postseason in the fourth. The strikes were quick and efficient, enough to let the Royals play, for the first time this postseason, from ahead. Eric Hosmer had an RBI double in the eighth, and Kendrys Morales added a sacrifice fly, enough to let Luke Hochevar close with a five-run lead.

Each run mattered, for the Blue Jays leave scant margin for error. They exhaust pitchers with their restraint. They embarrass them with their brawn. They wallop mistakes. They shatter the confidence of their foes.

The Royals proved last series, if any doubt lingered after 2014, how well they could absorb a punch.

Few opponents throw heavier blows than Toronto. The Blue Jays led the major leagues in runs, home runs, on-base percentage and slugging percentage. The heart of their order features three right-handed bombardiers: Donaldson, Bautista and Edwin Encarnacion.

To suppress the Jays, the Royals handed the baseball to Volquez. He amped his fastball up to 97 mph during a scoreless first inning that still required 24 pitches. Volquez balanced that with a six-pitch second.

Escobar could not advance after a leadoff double in the first. Two innings later, he came to the plate with Alex Gordon at second base. Gordon had ended a nine-pitch clash with right-hander Marco Estrada by doubling on a fastball into right field.

Now Escobar ripped at a curveball from Estrada. The pitch bent down and away, perhaps a strike, perhaps not. Escobar flicked it into right for a run-scoring double. When Estrada fired a elevated fastball two at-bats later, Lorenzo Cain shuttled an RBI single into right.

Two days before, Bautista hit a towering home run to clinch a Game 5 ALDS comeback over Texas. He flung his bat skyward, exhilarating the crowd at Rogers Centre and sparking an industrywide debate on the ethics of bat flips. Bautista can generate attention with either the reverberations of his bat or the bark of his voice.

Around the game, Bautista carries a reputation for chirping at umpires. The strike zone of Tony Randazzo aggravated him in the fourth. On two consecutive pitches, Randazzao rewarded Volquez with a high strike on the outside corner. After the second, Bautista waved his arms and stomped out of the batter's box. He returned in time to watch a curveball for strike three.

Perez came to the plate with two outs in the fourth. The previous two hitters had just struck out. Estrada fed Perez a 90-mph fastball at the belt. Perez made the baseball disappear over the left-field fence.

When the sixth inning rolled around, Volquez stood unchallenged. Yet on their third at-bats, neither Donaldson nor Bautista chased Volquez's pitches. Donaldson drained Volquez with a nine-pitch walk. He missed sinkers up in the zone but declined to hack at off-speed pitches out of his reach.

Donaldson trotted to first. The bullpen phone rang. Herrera hopped up.

Bautista repeated the pattern. He could not punish Volquez for misplaced fastballs. Volquez abandoned the heater for his change-up. He missed on the ninth pitch of the plate appearance and put Bautista on.

A figure emerged from the Royals dugout. It was not Yost. It was pitching coach Dave Eiland. He spoke with Volquez and left to watch him face Encarnacion.

By now, each encounter felt like trench warfare. Volquez could not command his fastball, but Encarnacion fouled off two juicy ones. He stared at a third for a critical out. The two-seamer dived at the last moment to catch the outer edge of the zone.

Up came first baseman Chris Colabello, who owned one of the two hits against Volquez. Colabello ripped the eighth pitch he saw into left. Gordon caught it.

The midseason arrival of shortstop Troy Tulowitzki coincided with the revival of the Blue Jays. Now he arrived in this game's moment of truth, only a month removed from a broken scapula that sidelined him in September.

Volquez elected to challenge the damaged star. He flung seven consecutive fastballs. The last clocked at 95 mph and hummed over the plate. Tulowitzki let it pass. The crowd erupted as Randazzo pumped his fist.

JOHN SLEEZER

Royals shortstop Alcides Escobar fired the ball to second for a force-out and the second out of the ninth inning of a 5-0 win over the Blue Jays.

Salvador Perez is checked on by home plate umpire Tony Randazzo after Perez was struck in the hand by a bat in the eighth inning.

JILL TOYOSHIBA

Story of the game

BY PETE GRATHOFF

1 Can't take advantage

Edinson Volquez opened the game with a strikeout of Ben Revere, who took a called third strike. The pitch showed nasty movement that fooled Revere. Jose Bautista walked with two outs, but Edwin Encarnacion grounded into a fielder's choice. Alcides Escobar opened the Royals' half with a double, but the Royals failed to score.

0-0
KC-TOR

2 All is quiet

After needing 24 pitches to get through the first inning, Volquez set the Blue Jays down in order on just a half-dozen pitches. The Royals went down in order, and the score remained the same.

0-0
KC-TOR

3 Royals take the lead

Toronto made its first bit of noise as Kevin Pillar walked and took second on Ryan Goins' sacrifice bunt. Pillar never advanced from there. Alex Gordon doubled down the the right-field line in the Royals' half and scored on a one-out double by Escobar. After Ben Zobrist grounded out, Lorenzo Cain laced a single to right and made it 2-0.

2-0
KC-TOR

4 Boom goes the dynamite

Chris Colabello's two-out single was the Blue Jays' first hit of the game and the first the Royals had allowed since the second inning of Game 5 of the ALDS. Volquez brushed it aside and struck out Troy Tulowitzki on a change-up. Kendrys Morales and Mike Moustakas struck out for the Royals, but Salvador Perez launched a solo shot to left-center field on the first pitch from Marco Estrada, and the packed house at Kauffman Stadium gave its resounding approval.

3-0
KC-TOR

5 Volquez humming along

Goins hit a clean single with two outs, but it mattered little as Revere grounded out to Moustakas at third base. The Royals didn't do anything in their half of the inning, going down in order.

3-0
KC-TOR

6 "Eddie, Eddie!"

Volquez ran into his first bit of trouble as Josh Donaldson and Bautista walked to start the inning. But Volquez seemed to be energized by the Kauffman crowd, which began chanting "Eddie, Eddie," and he struck out Encarnacion and got Colabello to fly to Gordon in left. His 111th and final pitch of the night caught Tulowitzki looking as Volquez escaped the jam. The Royals missed a chance to pad their lead when Eric Hosmer reached on a one-out error by Donaldson and moved to third on a single by Morales. But Moustakas hit into a 4-6-3 double play that ended the inning. It was started on a slick play by Goins at second base. Moustakas hit a slow chopper past the mound, but Goins rushed in and tossed to Tulowitzki, who made a smooth turn.

3-0
KC-TOR

7 Herrera wows everyone

Unfortunately for Toronto, this likely won't be the only appearance for Royals relief pitcher Kelvin Herrera. He needed just nine pitches to get two strikeouts and a harmless pop-up to Zobrist at second base. All nine were strikes. The Royals didn't get on base in their half, but with a three-run lead that didn't matter.

3-0
KC-TOR

8 And ... breathe

Ryan Madson replaced Herrera and got in a bit of a spot. With one out, Donaldson singled and Bautista was hit by a pitch. But Madson buckled down. Pinch hitter Justin Smoak popped up to Hosmer in foul ground near first, and Colabello grounded into a fielder's choice. Crisis averted. Toronto reliever LaTroy Hawkins hit Escobar with a pitch, and Zobrist reached on an infield single. After an out, Hosmer missed a homer to right by maybe 2 feet and Escobar sped home. Morales hit a sacrifice fly that scored Zobrist.

5-0
KC-TOR

9 Hochevar closes it out

No save situation, so Luke Hochevar finished out the game. He got Tulowitzki on an easy grounder to Moustakas at third. Moose made an error on a ball by the next batter, but Hochevar got an out on a fielder's choice and a fly ball to left.

5-0
KC-TOR

ROYALS 5, BLUE JAYS 0

Toronto	AB	R	H	BI	BB	SO	Avg.
Revere lf	4	0	0	0	0	1	.000
Donaldson 3b	3	0	1	0	1	0	.333
Bautista rf	1	0	0	0	3	1	.000
Encarnacion dh	3	0	0	0	0	1	.000
a-Smoak ph-dh	1	0	0	0	0	0	.000
Colabello 1b	4	0	1	0	0	0	.250
Tulowitzki ss	4	0	0	0	0	2	.000
D.Navarro c	4	0	0	0	0	1	.000
Pillar cf	3	0	0	0	1	0	.000
Goins 2b	3	0	1	0	0	1	.333
Totals	30	0	3	0	5	7	

Kansas City	AB	R	H	BI	BB	SO	Avg.
A.Escobar ss	3	2	2	1	0	0	.667
Zobrist 2b	4	1	1	0	0	0	.250
L.Cain cf	4	0	1	1	0	1	.250
Hosmer 1b	4	0	1	1	0	0	.250
K.Morales dh	3	0	1	1	0	2	.333
Moustakas 3b	4	0	0	0	0	2	.000
S.Perez c	3	1	1	1	0	0	.333
A.Gordon lf	3	1	1	0	0	0	.333
Rios rf	3	0	0	0	0	2	.000
Orlando rf	0	0	0	0	0	0	---
Totals	31	5	8	5	0	7	

Toronto	000	000	000	—	0	3 1
Kansas City	002	100	02x	—	5	8 1

E: Donaldson (1), Moustakas (1). **LOB:** Toronto 9, Kansas City 4. **2B:** A.Escobar 2 (2), Hosmer (1), A.Gordon (1). **HR:** S.Perez (1), off Estrada. **RBIs:** A.Escobar (1), L.Cain (1), Hosmer (1), K.Morales (1), S.Perez (1). **SB:** L.Cain (1). **S:** Goins. **SF:** K.Morales.

Runners left in scoring position: Toronto 3 (Donaldson, Tulowitzki, Colabello); Kansas City 4 (Hosmer 2, Moustakas 2). **RISP:** Toronto 0 for 7; Kansas City 3 for 12. **Runners moved up:** Zobrist. **GIDP:** Moustakas. **DP:** Toronto 1 (Goins, Tulowitzki, Colabello).

Toronto	IP	H	R	ER	BB	SO	NP	ERA
Estrada L, 0-1	5⅓	6	3	3	0	6	90	5.06
Loup	⅔	0	0	0	0	2		0.00
Lowe	1	0	0	0	1	1	12	0.00
Hawkins	1	2	2	2	0	0	14	18.00

Kansas City	IP	H	R	ER	BB	SO	NP	ERA
Volquez W, 1-0	6	2	0	0	4	5	111	0.00
K.Herrera	1	0	0	0	0	2	9	0.00
Madson	1	1	0	0	1	0	18	0.00
Hochevar	1	0	0	0	0	0	13	0.00

Holds: K.Herrera (1), Madson (1). **Inherited runners-scored:** Loup 2-0. **HBP:** by Hawkins (A.Escobar).

Umpires: Home, Tony Randazzo; First, Laz Diaz; Second, John Hirschbeck; Third, Hunter Wendelstedt; Left, Dan Iassogna; Right, Jeff Nelson. **Time:** 3:15. **Att:** 39,753.

JOHN SLEEZER

Perez powers up KC's bats

His solo homer is the Royals' ninth in six postseason games

The ninth home run of the Royals' postseason came on a 90-mph fastball that sat in the heart of the strike zone. It was the kind of pitch you don't want to throw to Salvador Perez. Especially with two outs in the bottom of the fourth.

As the baseball reached the plate, Perez timed the offering and unleashed a mighty hack. The baseball landed in a camera bay in left-center field, bouncing up against a Sonic sign and sending Kauffman Stadium into a moment of pure bliss.

Two days earlier, Kendrys Morales had capped a Game 5 victory over the Houston Astros with a three-run blast. That five-game series had been marked by power from both sides; Alex Gordon, Eric Hosmer and Lorenzo Cain each collected a homer during two games in Houston.

During the regular season, the Royals ranked 24th in the majors in homers, hitting 139 in 162 games. The Blue Jays, meanwhile, led all teams in clout, crushing 232 homers and scoring a major-league-best 891 runs.

That was the regular season. In six games in these playoffs, the Royals have drilled nine home runs. The Blue Jays have hit eight.

In the bottom of the eighth Friday, Hosmer came to the plate with two on and roped an RBI double off the top of the wall in right field. It was inches away from Kansas City's 10th home run, and as Hosmer stood at second base with a double, he twirled his finger around and looked back toward the Royals' dugout.

For a moment, Hosmer thought it was gone. It was not. And for the Royals, that was fine.

- Rustin Dodd

Kansas City Royals players celebrated their 5-0 victory in the American League Championship Series Game 1.

When Royals catcher Salvador Perez dumped a water bucket on starting pitcher Edinson Volquez, he also got Fox Sports commentator Ken Rosenthal.

It was a rare sight to see Royals left fielder Alex Gordon punch the air after his RBI double with two outs drove in the go-ahead run in the seventh inning Saturday.

ALLISON LONG

ALCS GAME 2

	123	456	789	R	H	E
Toronto	001	002	000	— 3	10	0
Kansas City	000	000	51x	— 6	8	0

     W W 3 4 5 6 7

THE KANSAS CITY STAR

10/18/2015

O ... M ... G!

....

The Royals score five runs in the seventh inning to beat the Blue Jays 6-3

....

Toronto's David Price allows just one hit in six innings before faltering

....

————————

BY ANDY McCULLOUGH

By now, their instincts are keen. The Royals spend enough time with blood on their chins to deduce the scent when an opponent is cut. When presented with an inch, this team makes plans for taking a mile.

So when Ben Zobrist's lazy fly ball fell into the outfield grass at Kauffman Stadium, their ears perked up. For six innings the team lay dormant, stilled by the left arm of Toronto ace David Price, who had retired 18 batters in a row. Now, in the climactic inning of a 6-3 victory Saturday, their minds operated as one.

"You know we've got something brewing," said Eric Hosmer, who drove in the Royals' first run two batters after Zobrist's hit.

"It opened the door for us to do what we do," said Mike Moustakas, who tied the game with a single of his own.

"Once this lineup gets moving, it's one guy after another," said Alex Gordon, who gave his team its first lead with an RBI double. "And it was a big seventh inning."

The rally resulted in five runs, enough to ruin a performance from Price that looked as if it might border on historic. The psychic blow to Toronto cannot be considered fatal - the Blue Jays already rallied from an 0-2 series deficit once this postseason. Yet, the Royals have announced themselves, once again, and stand two victories away from a return to the World Series.

In the last 18 innings, the Royals stared down the Blue Jays,

SHANE KEYSER

An ocean of blue swelled with elation as first baseman Eric Hosmer slid home as the tying run during the Royals' seventh-inning rally against Toronto at Kauffman Stadium.

those swaggering brutes from the Great White North, and refused to blink.

On Friday, their pitching staff turned baseball's most lethal group of hitters into a whimpering collection of outs. A day later, the offense tarnished the reputation of Toronto's ace. In the process, the Royals demonstrated the depth of their talent and the sturdiness of their chins.

"Our guys, they never quit," manager Ned Yost said. "They just keep going."

A split looked likely when Saturday's seventh started. Price gave up a single to Alcides Escobar on the game's first pitch. He did not let another Royal reach base until Zobrist benefited from miscommunication by second baseman Ryan Goins and right fielder José Bautista.

"David was so good tonight that it was a shame it had to end that way," Toronto manager John Gibbons said.

The Royals have made laments like this sound routine. The franchise shifted into a new era after the raucous win in last year's AL Wild Card Game. This year's team spoiled an upstart bid from Houston with its season-saving comeback in Game 4 of the last round. So a three-run deficit with three innings to go, even against a dynamic performer like Price, falls within their range of expectation.

In the sixth inning, Yost went to the mound to fetch starter Yordano Ventura. For five innings, Ventura offered a reasonable counterweight to Price. Two doubles led to a third-inning run, but otherwise Ventura kept the Blue Jays at bay. But he lost his footing in the sixth.

During a 31-pitch effort, Ventura gave up an infield single to third baseman Josh Donaldson and walked Bautista. Playing with an injured hand, Edwin Encarnacion hit an RBI single that ticked off Escobar's glove. Troy Tulowitzki added a run-scoring double on an opposite-field liner that just evaded the glove of right fielder Alex Rios.

At the mound, before he handed the ball to Luke Hochevar, Yost consoled Ventura.

"I'm like, look, we're going to get you off the hook here," Yost said.

A passionate performance

SHANE KEYSER

SHANE KEYSER

SHANE KEYSER

You could tell from his expressions that the Blue Jays were starting to get to Royals starter Yordano Ventur in the sixth inning, but he still managed to keep his team in the game.

The task sounded tall. Up to that point, Price appeared on the brink of his first postseason victory as a starter. As the innings progressed, the hulking exterior of the stadium cast a shadow across the diamond.

"The shadows were really tough," center fielder Lorenzo Cain said. "I felt like the ball was disappearing the first few innings."

Price gave up a leadoff single to Escobar and then proceeded to devastate the Royals.

"Price is a tough pitcher," Gordon said. "I felt like we needed to catch a break."

The seventh provided one. Zobrist popped up the first pitch he saw from Price. He slammed his bat as the ball drifted into right.

"I didn't think there was a chance that ball dropped," Zobrist said.

Goins and Bautista converged on the ball. Goins waved his glove toward Bautista. At the last moment, Goins stopped, causing his momentum to send him tumbling to his backside. The baseball soon joined him in the grass.

"I just thought I heard, 'I got it,' but it was nothing," Goins said. "I should have gone in more aggressively. I put my glove up, like I always do. That means I got it. I just didn't make the play."

From there, the Royals' offensive machine hummed to life.

Cain singled, which stoked the crowd at Kauffman Stadium. Hosmer dug out a change-up, low and away, and punched it into left for Kansas City's first run. First-base coach Rusty Kuntz instructed Hosmer to swipe second base, even though Price had not allowed a stolen base all season.

Hosmer barreled into second as Kendrys Morales hit a grounder up the middle. A run scored. Only one out was recorded.

"The key to that whole inning, believe it or not, was Hosmer stealing second base," Yost said. "That was a double-play ball. That allowed us to get to a point we could score five runs. That was huge."

Up came Moustakas, who had only one hit in nine career at-bats against Price. Price tried a change-up low in the zone. Moustakas ripped it into right, toward Bautista and his powerful right arm.

Neither Hosmer nor third-base coach Mike Jirschele fretted about Bautista. Jirschele flailed his arm to send the tying run home from second.

"It didn't matter if he stopped me or what," Hosmer said. "I was going either way."

Bautista's throw sprayed away from catcher Russell Martin. Hosmer arrived safely.

After Salvador Perez struck out, Gordon hammered a fastball down the heart of the plate for the go-ahead double.

SHANE KEYSER

Royals shortstop Alcides Escobar tossed a ball to second base that he caught off a hit by Blue Jays catcher Russell Martin in the second inning to complete a double play.

Story of the game

BY PETE GRATHOFF

1 Royals win replay challenge
Yordano Ventura breezed through the opening inning, inducing a ground-out before striking out Public Enemy No. 2, Josh Donaldson. The boos increased when Jose Bautista came to the plate, but he grounded out. Alcides Escobar opened the Royals' half with a single (of course he did), but Ben Zobrist hit into a fielder's choice. It was initially ruled a double play, but the Royals challenged and won. Lorenzo Cain flied to center and Eric Hosmer struck out.

0-0
KC-TOR

2 Escobar's gem
Edwin Encarnacion and Chris Colabello hit consecutive singles, and the Blue Jays appeared to be in business. However, Ventura struck out Troy Tulowitzki. Russell Martin hit a line drive toward short. Encarnacion ducked while running and the ball shot over him, but Escobar made a splendid diving catch and flipped to Zobrist for the double play. The Royals didn't hit the ball out of the infield against David Price.

0-0
KC-TOR

3 Double-double
Kevin Pillar's fly to right-center just eluded the grasp of Alex Rios to start the inning. Ryan Goins, who was hitting .050 in the playoffs, didn't bunt. Instead he ripped a run-scoring double past Mike Moustakas down the left-field line. The Royals didn't have a base runner against Price in their half of the frame.

1-0
TOR-KC

4 Price is right on
Tulowitzki's two-out single just cleared Escobar, who ran into short left field and made a jumping attempt at a catch - with his bare hand. Nothing came of it as Russell Martin grounded to third. Meanwhile, Price continued to make short work of the Royals. Strikeouts of Zobrist and Hosmer were sandwiched around Cain's ground-out to short.

1-0
TOR-KC

5 Royals make contact
Ventura had no trouble with Pillar and Goins this time around, recording a pop-up and a strikeout. Ben Revere hit a ball hard to left, but it was right at Alex Gordon. The Royals didn't have a hit, but it was their best inning against Price. Kendrys Morales smashed a bullet to third baseman Donaldson,

Moustakas hit a ball well to center, and Perez's grounder to short had some speed behind it.

1-0
TOR-KC

6 Jays pad their lead
Ventura threw 31 pitches in the inning, giving up three hits and two walks with one strikeout. Two runs had scored, and Toronto had the bases loaded when Luke Hochevar relieved. He got Pillar to pop up to Zobrist and Goins to ground to Hosmer. Price had his best inning, striking out the side.

3-0
TOR-KC

7 Price is wrong
Danny Duffy set down Revere on a grounder to short, Donaldson on a fly to center and struck out Bautista looking. Zobrist popped up starting the bottom of the inning and slammed his bat in disgust. It was premature. Goins went back from second base and Bautista came in from right and the ball fell between them thanks to a miscommunication. Who knew that was the match that would light the fuse? Here's what followed: Cain single, Hosmer RBI single, Morales RBI ground-out, Moustakas RBI single, Perez strikeout and an Alex Gordon RBI double. That finished Price, and Aaron Sanchez relieved. Rios drilled a single that scored Gordon, and the Royals had a 5-3 lead.

5-3
KC-TOR

8 Moose delivers
Kelvin Herrera wasn't as dominating as in Game 1, but he wasn't fazed by a one-out double by Colabello. Tulowitzki flied out to right, and Martin struck out. Cain drew a one-out walk but was caught stealing after Aaron Loup came on to pitch. Hosmer and Morales then drew consecutive walks, and Moustakas laced a single to right that scored Hosmer.

6-3
KC-TOR

9 The Wade Davis Experience
Toronto showed some fight as Pillar singled off Wade Davis and pinch hitter Cliff Pennington walked on a 3-2 pitch. But Davis struck out Revere and Donaldson. Bautista flied out harmlessly to right field. And there was much joy at Kauffman Stadium.

6-3
KC-TOR

ROYALS 6, BLUE JAYS 3

Toronto	AB	R	H	BI	BB	SO	Avg.
Revere lf	5	0	0	0	0	2	.000
Donaldson 3b	5	1	1	0	0	2	.250
Bautista rf	4	1	0	0	1	1	.000
Encarnacion dh	4	0	2	1	0	2	.286
Colabello 1b	4	0	2	0	0	1	.375
Tulowitzki ss	4	0	2	1	0	1	.250
Ru.Martin c	3	0	0	0	1	1	.000
Pillar cf	4	1	2	0	0	0	.286
Goins 2b	3	0	1	1	0	1	.333
a-Pennington ph	0	0	0	0	1	0	---
Totals	36	3	10	3	3	11	

Kansas City	AB	R	H	BI	BB	SO	Avg.
A.Escobar ss	4	0	1	0	0	1	.429
Zobrist 2b	4	1	1	0	0	1	.250
L.Cain cf	3	1	1	0	1	0	.286
Hosmer 1b	3	2	1	1	1	2	.286
K.Morales dh	3	0	0	1	1	1	.167
Moustakas 3b	4	1	2	2	0	0	.250
S.Perez c	4	0	0	0	0	1	.143
A.Gordon lf	3	1	1	1	0	1	.333
Rios rf	3	0	1	1	0	1	.167
1-Orlando pr-rf	0	0	0	0	0	0	---
Totals	31	6	8	6	3	8	

Toronto	001	002	000	— 3	10 0
Kansas City	000	000	51x	— 6	8 0

a-walked for Goins in the 9th.
1-ran for Rios in the 7th.
LOB: Toronto 9, Kansas City 4. **2B:** Colabello (1), Tulowitzki (1), Pillar (1), Goins (1), A.Gordon (2). **RBIs:** Encarnacion (1), Tulowitzki (1), Goins (1), Hosmer (2), K.Morales (2), Moustakas 2 (2), A.Gordon (1), Rios (1). **CS:** L.Cain (1).
Runners left in scoring position: Toronto 5 (Bautista 2, Goins 2, Ru.Martin); Kansas City 1 (S.Perez). **RISP:** Toronto 3 for 16; Kansas City 5 for 8. **Runners moved up:** Donaldson, K.Morales. **DP:** Kansas City 1 (A.Escobar, Zobrist).

Toronto	IP	H	R	ER	BB	SO	NP	ERA
Price L, 0-1	6⅔	6	5	5	0	8	96	6.75
Aa.Sanchez	⅔	1	0	0	1	0	15	0.00
Loup	⅓	1	1	1	2	0	12	9.00
Lowe	⅓	0	0	0	0	0	4	0.00

Kansas City	IP	H	R	ER	BB	SO	NP	ERA
Ventura	5⅓	8	3	3	2	6	97	5.06
Hochevar	⅔	0	0	0	0	0	5	0.00
D.Duffy W, 1-0	1	0	0	0	0	1	16	0.00
K.Herrera	1	1	0	0	0	2	11	0.00
W.Davis S, 1	1	1	0	0	1	2	20	0.00

Holds: K.Herrera (2). **Inherited runners-scored:** Aa.Sanchez 1-1, Loup 1-0, Lowe 2-0, Hochevar 3-0.
Umpires: Home, Laz Diaz; First, John Hirschbeck; Second, Hunter Wendelstedt; Third, Dan Iassogna; Left, Jeff Nelson; Right, Tony Randazzo. **Time:** 3:19. **Att:** 40,357.

Moustakas swings out of slump

Royals third baseman comes through against Toronto ace David Price

The sight of Toronto ace David Price can turn the best left-handed hitters in the world to jelly-legged chum. The arsenal of Price - all cantilever windup and baffling pitch sequences and disappearing change-up - can be devastating. And on an afternoon like Saturday, when the shadows are creeping and Price is dealing, you just never know.

"You can't guess what he's going to throw," said Royals second baseman Ben Zobrist, who spent seven seasons playing behind Price in Tampa Bay.

As Mike Moustakas strode to the plate in the seventh inning Saturday he understood this Price maxim better than most. In nine career at-bats against Price - including two earlier in the day - he had collected one hit and struck out three times. Mired in an 0-for-13 skid, Moustakas dug in with a runner on second base and the Royals trailing by a single run in Game 2 of the American League Championship Series.

There could be no guessing, only reacting, and after fighting off an onslaught of four straight fastballs, Moustakas's eyes read change-up, fading toward the outer half of the plate. He didn't miss.

Moustakas rapped a sharp single to right field, scoring Eric Hosmer from second base - thanks to a wise decision from third-base coach Mike Jirschele - and sending another message in the Royals' 6-3 victory over the Toronto Blue Jays. No hitter can survive a slump quite like Moustakas, who busted out for two hits, two RBIs and a run scored after beginning the postseason in a prolonged funk.

"We never give up," Moustakas said. "We never stop fighting. And we always think that, no matter how many innings are left, as long as we have some outs left, we're going to find a way to win."

- Rustin Dodd

Catcher Salvador Perez made a bare-handed catch on a foul pop-up by Toronto Blue Jays third baseman Josh Donaldson in the sixth inning but the hitter was not called out because the ball hit a wire that supports the backstop net on its way down.

Center fielder Lorenzo Cain drove a single to right field that ignited a five-run rally in the seventh inning of Game 2.

Toronto Blue Jays second baseman Ryan Goins sat on the ground and looked at the ball after he waved right fielder Jose Bautista off on a fly ball hit by Kansas City Royals second baseman Ben Zobrist in the seventh inning. Zobrist singled on the play.

SHANE KEYSER

SHANE KEYSER

Kansas City Royals first baseman Eric Hosmer celebrated with designated hitter Kendrys Morales after Hosmer scored on a single by third baseman Mike Moustakas to tie up the game 3-3.

JOHN SLEEZER

Alex Gordon got a chest bump from Eric Hosmer in the seventh inning as the Blue Jays changed pitchers after Gordon knocked in the go-ahead run.

Kansas City Royals first baseman Eric Hosmer had a bloodied lip after he got smacked in the mouth by a foul ball he hit in the fifth inning.

JOHN SLEEZER

ALCS GAME 3

	123	456	789	R	H	E
Kansas City	101	020	004 —	8	10	0
Toronto	036	010	01x —	11	8	0

W W L 4 5 6 7

THE KANSAS CITY STAR

10/20/2015

No Royal welcome

Hammered hard, KC starter Cueto hears it from fans after early exit

Royals score four in ninth but end up losing 11-8 as Jays make it a 2-1 series

BY ANDY McCULLOUGH

TORONTO

The injury still stung, a deep, lasting bruise left after Toronto's slumbering python awakened and loosened the Kansas City stranglehold around its neck.

Now came the insults, thousands of them, flying from every angle inside Rogers Centre in the third inning of an 11-8 Royals loss to Toronto in Game 3 of the American League Championship Series.

As a group of shell-shocked Royals circled the mound, starter Johnny Cueto handed the ball to manager Ned Yost. It was a move some would argue should have occurred three batters earlier, before Cueto surrendered a series-altering, three-run homer to Troy Tulowitzki. A frothing crowd erupted with cheers, mirthful but cruel, as Cueto shuffled toward the dugout.

Cueto could not ignore the noise. He gazed up at the fans pointing and shouting at him. And then he did the oddest thing: He smiled. He craned his neck at the wall of bodies clad in blue and white. He cast his eyes downward but still the expression pocked his face.

During three months as a Royal, his behavior continues to confound.

Cueto could not repeat the frenetic pace and brazen aggressiveness from his last start, Game 5 of the American League Division Series, when he retired the last 19 Astros he faced. On Monday he faced 17 batters. Only six made outs. He ceded the stage to Kris Medlen, who gave up two runs but still saved the bullpen.

The struggles of Cueto and Medlen ruined another relentless

Royals starting pitcher Johnny Cueto walked off the field after being relieved in the third inning.

JOHN SLEEZER

evening from the offense. When Kendrys Morales boomed a two-run homer in the ninth inning against closer Roberto Osuna, the Royals trimmed the lead to three. But they could only offset so much failure on the mound.

Cueto dueled with Marcus Stroman, a 24-year-old right-hander only seven months removed from surgery to repair a torn anterior cruciate ligament in his left knee.

Stroman exuded youthful exuberance as he warmed up before the game, slapping five with fans along the left-field line as the stands filled.

Stroman fell victim to a curious condition afflicting American League pitchers this October: He threw Alcides Escobar a strike. Escobar swung through the game's first pitch, an inside fastball, but flicked the second into right field toward José Bautista.

Bautista tumbled to the turf in an attempt for acrobatics. The decision was misguided. The baseball bounced behind him, and Escobar raced to third. He scored on a ground-out by Ben Zobrist.

The two halves of the first inning offered a study in contrasts. The Royals saw seven pitches and scored a run. The Blue Jays forced Cueto to throw 25 and came up empty.

The rowdies at Rogers Centre enlivened Cueto. He received a fierce round of boos when he was introduced before the game. With his smile beaming across the center-field scoreboard, he tipped his cap and waved to the angry throng.

To rattle Cueto, the fans relied upon the script written in Pittsburgh during the 2013 National League Wild Card Game. The two syllables can sound like an expletive when elongated and spat outward on pipes lubricated by Labatt Blue. The chants rained down upon him from the start, and Cueto flashed a grin and popped bubblegum inside his jaw.

The smile disappeared in the second inning. Cueto yielded a one-out single to shortstop Tulowitzki, who looked compromised earlier this postseason by the crack in his scapula. Next Cueto smoked catcher Russell Martin with a fastball. The force caused Martin's left wrist guard to unravel and fall into the dirt.

Cueto soon completed a similar journey. He produced a groundball off the bat of Kevin Pillar. Escobar fed Zobrist for one out, but Zobrist could not turn two in time. Pillar soon jetted to second base, which was unoccupied. Both plays cost the Royals.

At the moment, the extra 90 feet for Pillar mattered little. There were two outs and Cueto was facing No. 9 hitter Ryan Goins, who came to the plate with an .087 batting average in the playoffs. Cueto kept aiming for belt-high strikes, but umpire John Hirschbeck did not cooperate.

On the ninth pitch of the at-bat, Goins stroked a single into left. Tulowitzki scored and Pillar sprinted just inches ahead of the tag after a throw by Alex Gordon.

The singsong jeering continued as Cueto walked Ben Revere and watched Josh Donaldson smash an RBI single past the dive of Mike Moustakas.

Kansas City cut into Toronto's lead with a run in the third. But Cueto imploded in the bottom of the inning. From the start, he looked troubled. All four pitches he threw to Edwin Encarnacion rose in the upper register of the strike zone. Cueto gave up a single, and then walked first baseman Chris Colabello.

The revival of Tulowitzki began in Game 2, when he notched a pair of hits. Now he came to the plate with the evening hanging in the balance. Before Game 5 against Houston, the Royals vowed to remove Cueto at the first sign of danger. The combination of his dominance that night and the games scheduled for Tuesday and Wednesday afforded Cueto more leeway in this contest.

Cueto did not reward the Royals for their faith. The bullpen mounds were unoccupied as Cueto fed Tulowitzki a 93-mph fastball near the letters. Center fielder Lorenzo Cain sprinted toward the wall, only to run out of room. Tulowitzki pointed at his dugout as he galloped along the bases.

Only now did the bullpen activate. Medlen warmed up as Cueto's night stumbled to a conclusion. He walked Martin. For his final act, Cueto served up a ringing RBI double to Pillar. At last Yost emerged for the merciful removal.

A few minutes later, as Medlen went to work, the crowd bemoaned the departure of Kansas City's woebegone ace.

"We want Cueto," they shouted. "We want Cueto."

The mocking did not arrive without merit. Cueto is not scheduled to pitch again in this series until Game 7. Toronto can only hope for another crack at him.

JILL TOYOSHIBA

Kansas City Royals shortstop Alcides Escobar gets a triple off Toronto Blue Jays starting pitcher Marcus Stroman in the first inning in Toronto.

JOHN SLEEZER

Relief pitcher Kris Medlen got a new ball for his next pitch while the Jays' Ryan Goins rounded the bases after hitting a solo homer in the fifth inning.

Story of the game

1 Seven significant pitches
Of course, Alcides Escobar swung at the first pitch from Marcus Stroman. He didn't make contact but did with the second, lining a ball that got past right fielder Jose Bautista, who played it poorly. Escobar sped to third and scored on the next pitch when Ben Zobrist grounded out to second. Lorenzo Cain hit a laser to the wall at center, but Kevin Pillar made a sensational catch. Eric Hosmer grounded out and, whew, all that happened on just seven pitches. Johnny Cueto issued a two-out walk to Bautista, then struck out Edwin Encarnacion.

1-0
KC-TOR

2 Blue Jays pull ahead
The Royals got two singles (Kendrys Morales leading off and Alex Gordon with two outs), but Alex Rios flied out to right. Troy Tulowitzki had a one-out single for Toronto, and Russell Martin was hit by a pitch. Pillar grounded into a fielder's choice, barely avoiding a double play, and then stole second. Ryan Goins lined a single to left that scored Tulowitzki and Pillar, who made a nice slide to avoid a tag at the plate. Ben Revere walked, and Josh Donaldson singled past Mike Moustakas at third and Goins scored.

3-1
TOR-KC

3 Cueto's short night
Zobrist doubled with one out and took third on Cain's infield single. Hosmer grounded to first and Cain was forced out, but Hosmer avoided the double play with a headfirst slide into first as Zobrist scored. The Blue Jays then knocked out Cueto. Encarnacion singled, Chris Colabello walked, and Tulowitzki hit a three-run homer over the center-field wall. Martin followed with a walk and scored on Pillar's double. Kris Medlen entered, got a couple of outs and then allowed a homer to Donaldson.

9-2
TOR-KC

4 Take a breath...
The Royals went down in order, and the Blue Jays got a leadoff single from Encarnacion, but Colabello hit into a double play and Tulowitzki struck out.

9-2
TOR-KC

5 Two for one
The Royals made some noise again. Escobar singled and moved to third on Zobrist's double. Cain flied out, but Escobar scored on a wild pitch. After Hosmer struck out, Morales walked, and Moustakas delivered an RBI single. Toronto struck back on a two-out home run from Goins.

10-4
TOR-KC

6 Base runners, but no runs
Escobar had a two-out single for the Royals, but the Royals came up empty. Bautista's one-out walk also didn't amount to anything for Toronto.

10-4
TOR-KC

7 Temper, temper
Hosmer had a one-out single, but there was to be no rally. Aaron Sanchez came into the game, and Morales flied out and Moustakas grounded out. Tulowitzki opened the inning by being called out on strikes. He wasn't happy. Martin was also rung up looking and Pillar flied out. When Tulowitzki came back onto the field after the inning, he apparently said something inappropriate to home-plate umpire John Hirschbeck and got the heave-ho.

10-4
TOR-KC

8 One more for Toronto
Reliever Mark Lowe entered for the Blue Jays and set down the Royals quickly, although Gordon seemed displeased about the strike zone. Franklin Morales took over for the Royals. With one out, Revere beat out an infield single, Donaldson walked, and Bautista got his first hit, a single to left that scored Revere.

11-4
TOR-KC

9 Royals don't go quietly
Liam Hendricks gave up a single to Escobar and Zobrist doubled. Cain's fly-out scored Escobar, and Hosmer had an RBI single. Toronto was forced to summon closer Roberto Osuna, and Kendrys Morales greeted him with a mammoth two-run homer to right-center. But that was as close as the Royals could get. Moustakas and Salvador Perez each grounded out, and the Jays had their first win of the series.

11-8
TOR-KC

BLUE JAYS 11, ROYALS 8

Kansas City	AB	R	H	BI	BB	SO	Avg.
Escobar ss	5	3	4	0	0	0	.583
Zobrist 2b	5	3	3	1	0	0	.385
Cain cf	4	0	1	1	0	0	.273
Hosmer 1b	5	1	2	2	0	1	.333
K.Morales dh	4	1	3	2	1	0	.400
Moustakas 3b	5	0	1	1	0	0	.231
Perez c	5	0	0	0	0	0	.083
Gordon lf	4	0	1	0	0	1	.300
Rios rf	4	0	0	0	0	0	.100
Totals	41	8	15	7	1	2	

Toronto	AB	R	H	BI	BB	SO	Avg.
Revere lf	4	1	1	0	1	0	.077
Donaldson 3b	4	1	2	3	1	1	.333
Bautista rf	3	0	1	1	2	1	.125
Encarnacion dh	5	1	2	0	0	2	.333
Colabello 1b	3	1	0	0	1	0	.273
Smoak 1b	1	0	0	0	0	0	.000
Tulowitzki ss	4	2	2	3	0	2	.333
Pennington 2b	0	0	0	0	0	0	—
Ru.Martin c	2	1	0	0	1	2	.000
Pillar cf	4	2	1	1	0	0	.273
Goins 2b-ss	4	2	2	3	0	1	.400
Totals	34	11	11	11	6	9	

Kansas City	101	020	004	—	8	15	0
Toronto	036	010	01x	—	11	11	0

LOB: Kansas City 8, Toronto 6. **2B:** Zobrist 3 (3), Pillar (2). **3B:** Escobar (1). **HR:** K.Morales (1), off Osuna; Tulowitzki (1), off Cueto; Donaldson (1), off Medlen; Goins (1), off Medlen. **RBIs:** Zobrist (1), Cain (2), Hosmer 2 (4), K.Morales 2 (4), Moustakas (3), Donaldson 3 (3), Bautista (1), Tulowitzki (4), Pillar (1), Goins 3 (4). **SB:** Pillar (1). **SF:** Cain.
Runners left in scoring position: Kansas City 3 (Rios, Moustakas, Perez); Toronto 2 (Bautista, Smoak). **RISP:** Kansas City 3 for 10; Toronto 5 for 11. **Runners moved up:** Zobrist. **GIDP:** Colabello. **DP:** Kansas City 1 (Zobrist, Escobar, Hosmer).

Kansas City	IP	H	R	ER	BB	SO	NP	ERA
Cueto L, 0-1	2	6	8	8	4	2	69	36.00
Medlen	5	3	2	2	1	6	70	3.60
F.Morales	1	2	1	1	1	1	20	9.00

Toronto	IP	H	R	ER	BB	SO	NP	ERA
Stroman W, 1-0	6⅓	11	4	4	1	1	94	5.68
Aa.Sanchez	⅔	0	0	0	0	0	12	0.00
Lowe	1	0	0	0	0	0	12	0.00
Hendriks	⅓	3	3	3	0	0	9	81.00
Osuna	⅔	1	1	1	0	0	9	13.50

Cueto pitched to 5 batters in the 3rd.
Inherited runners-scored: Medlen 1-1, Aa.Sanchez 1-0, Osuna 1-1. **HBP:** by Cueto (Ru.Martin). **WP:** Stroman.
Umpires: Home, John Hirschbeck; First, Hunter Wendelstedt; Second, Dan Iassogna; Third, Jeff Nelson; Left, Jim Reynolds; Right, Laz Diaz. **Time:** 3:13. **Att:** 49,751.

JOHN SLEEZER

Medlen saves bullpen after Cueto gets rocked

Reliever allows two earned runs and three hits in five innings of work

TORONTO

The bullpen door swung open, and out came Kris Medlen, breaking into a steady jog in the bottom of the third inning. Medlen had not been seen in 18 days. He had not pitched in a jubilant five-game series victory over the Houston Astros, and he was not needed for the first two games of the American League Championship Series at Kauffman Stadium.

That changed Monday night in Game 3, as Royals starter Johnny Cueto melted down in tremendous fashion in the early innings of an 11-8 loss to the Blue Jays at the Rogers Centre. With Cueto rendered ineffective, Royals manager Ned Yost turned to Medlen, who responded with a solid five-inning performance that saved the bullpen from a night of abuse.

Medlen showed little rust after nearly three weeks of inactivity. After entering with nobody out in the third, he recorded 15 outs and worked through the bottom of the seventh, allowing two earned runs and three hits. Medlen surrendered homers to Toronto's Josh Donaldson and Ryan Goins and allowed one inherited runner to score, but he also mixed in six strikeouts while issuing just one walk.

As the Blue Jays pulled within 2-1 in the series, Medlen kept the core of the Royals' bullpen fresh. Yost used left-hander Franklin Morales in the bottom of the eighth but kept Wade Davis, Kelvin Herrera, Ryan Madson and Danny Duffy in the bullpen for the duration of the night.

In that regard, Medlen came up big, leaving one question in the aftermath: When might we see Medlen again?

- Rustin Dodd

JOHN SLEEZER

Left fielder Alex Gordon walked back to the dugout after he struck out in the eighth inning.

SHANE KEYSER

Designated hitter Kendrys Morales hit a two-run homer in a ninth-inning rally that pulled the Royals within three runs of the Blue Jays.

Heckled without mercy by fans of his old team in Toronto, Alex Rios made his best catch of the season during Game 3 of the ALCS, sliding into the right-field corner to corral this pop fly.

Toronto Blue Jays center fielder Kevin Pillar dived for home plate past Kansas City Royals catcher Salvador Perez to score in the second inning on a two-RBI hit by second baseman Ryan Goins.

Tuesday's outcome had
Jarrod Dyson and Lorenzo
Cain jumping for joy, and
why not? The Royals' 14-2
victory at Toronto had them
one win away from a World
Series encore.

SHANE KEYSER

ALCS GAME 4

	1 2 3	4 5 6	7 8 9	R	H	E
Kansas City	410	000	432 —	14	15	0
Toronto	002	000	000 —	2	7	0

W W L W 5 6 7

THE KANSAS CITY STAR

10/21/2015

Blue crush

....

Royals flip the script on explosive Jays, 14-2

....

BY SAM MELLINGER

TORONTO

They shouted from the dugout to keep the line moving, because at some point that old baseball saw became their slogan. The easiest thing in the world is to adopt a saying and repeat it. The harder accomplishment is putting it into motion, turning it into reality, even pushing another unforgettable season to within one win of the World Series.

These Royals can be an overwhelming machine when the parts are in harmony, and for the last two years - finally - the parts have almost always been in harmony. Each of them has a story, some better known than others, all of them working together for the best baseball Kansas City has seen in a generation.

They beat the Blue Jays 14-2 in Game 4 of the American League Championship Series at the Rogers Centre on Tuesday, a whipping so complete that Blue Jays utilityman Cliff Pennington became the first position player to pitch a postseason game since at least 1914.

The Royals lead the series three games to one, with Game 5 Wednesday afternoon. They need to win just once in three tries to win another American League pennant.

"Ninth inning, two outs, me at third," Alex Gordon said, the memory of last year rushing back. "Just so close, and coming up short. That's the motivating factor."

They attacked the Blue Jays from the beginning, swinging early and often and hard, chasing starter R.A. Dickey in the second inning. Ben Zobrist hit a knuckleball over the fence. Lorenzo Cain stole a base and later scored on a passed ball.

Four more runs came in the seventh, three in the eighth, two in

the ninth. There was no referee to stop the fight, so the Royals just kept coming, and coming, then coming again, scoring runs long after they had squashed any remaining doubt from this game like a cigarette butt under a boot.

"Just a great overall team win," starting pitcher Chris Young said. "That's what this group is."

Fittingly, they did the closing damage with no home runs - eight singles, three walks, three run-scoring sacrifice flies, a double and a hit batter. When the Royals are right, they are more buckshot than bombs, winning the fight like a pack of dogs rather than one lion.

They have taken to calling this "frenzy hitting," another of those identifiers that might not make sense to outsiders but fits this group like an old slipper.

"It can come at any time," reliever Luke Hochevar said. "You just know these guys are going to fight every at-bat. They're going to battle every pitch."

The Blue Jays were the heavy betting favorite to win the World Series when these playoffs began and came into the ALCS on a wild show of force and bat-flipping against the Rangers in the ALDS.

JOHN SLEEZER

Kansas City Royals right fielder Alex Rios launched a solo home run into the sky in the second inning, then pointed to the sky on his trip home.

But the Royals just won a hinge game - now up 3-1 instead of tied 2-2 - by squishing the Blue Jays' bats and outslugging the world's baddest hitters. They scored 14 runs with 15 hits on Tuesday, numbers the Blue Jays matched only three times in 171 games, including this postseason.

The Royals are outscoring (33-16), outhitting (.331-.233) and outslugging (.496-.346) the Blue Jays in this series. Include the Division Series and the Royals hitters are still outperforming the Blue Jays. Starting with the eighth inning of Game 4 of the Division Series, they have scored 47 runs in 44 innings.

Back home, this has created an intoxicating and irresistible new passion. Kansas Citians have never watched or read this much about a baseball team, ever. They have never bought as many tickets, even back in the 1970s and 1980s, when the team always won and the games weren't on television as much.

Winning is the most important thing, of course. It always is. But there is something more about this team that has grabbed

Royals shortstop Alcides Escobar and second baseman Ben Zobrist met at home plate after Zobrist drove in Escobar with a home run in the first inning.

Escobar, Zobrist excel at setting the table

Shortstop bunts, second baseman homers, opening Game 4 of the ALCS

TORONTO
When the score stands at 2-0 two batters into the game, a team's table-setting skills are impeccable.

Those two runs at the outset set the game's tone and immediately wiped away the sour taste of the Royals' loss in Game 3.

Against knuckleballer R.A. Dickey, Alcides Escobar swung through the first pitch. As he stepped in the batter's box for the second, he took a quick glance at third base and saw Josh Donaldson playing deep and perfectly placed a bunt.

Up stepped Ben Zobrist, and out went the baseball - a home run launched into the stands that sucked the air out of the Rogers Centre.

"They've been table-setters.

They've been run producers. It's been fun to watch them go to work every day," Royals manager Ned Yost said.

Tuesday, Escobar chipped in a pair of sacrifice flies, Zobrist another base hit. Four games into the ALCS, Escobar is hitting .600 (9 for 15) and Zobrist .389 (7 for 18). If the series had ended Tuesday, or if it ends today, Escobar likely would be chosen series MVP.

On Monday, Escobar collected four hits and Zobrist three doubles, with each scoring three runs. Zobrist's output was a Royals' postseason record, and Escobar's four hits tied a club mark.

Through their two postseason series, the Royals are hitting .284 with 12 home runs - a record for a Royals' playoff year. Every regular except Escobar and Mike Moustakas has at least one home run, and Lorenzo Cain extended his postseason hitting streak to 13 games, a stretch that dates to last season.

"This whole team up and down the line - everybody feels dangerous right now," Zobrist said.

- Blair Kerkhoff

people back home. Some of that is in the stories, about Lorenzo Cain finding baseball only after being cut from the basketball team, or Alex Gordon's relentlessness, or Salvador Perez's interminable smile and toughness.

But there was a particularly special moment on Tuesday, one that people who have been around the team for a while surely noticed but others may have missed. It happened in the fifth inning, when Hochevar jogged in from the bullpen into the biggest out of the game to that point.

He came to the Royals as the only No. 1 overall pick in franchise history, technically made by the old leadership group, but in reality very much a part of what general manager Dayton Moore and his lieutenants were trying to build.

They saw in Hochevar a foundational piece, a future top-of-the-rotation starter for a franchise that had an agonizing time developing one in a sport that demanded at least a few. They spent seven years and gave Hochevar 128 big-league starts in chasing that vision. He was occasionally terrific, but the flashes were too short and rare, washed away with continued struggles.

Two years ago, the Royals made him a relief pitcher, and the results were both immediate and spectacular: He struck out 82 batters and walked just 17, posting a 1.92 ERA in 70⅓ innings. The Royals had a brand new weapon.

The next year his elbow gave out, and at least a few club officials admitted being choked up talking about the empathy they felt for a man who had finally found his place in baseball.

But Hochevar is back now, and statistics and scout opinions agree he has become stronger as the season has progressed. He is now their top reliever outside of the back-end triumvirate of Wade Davis, Ryan Madson and Kelvin Herrera.

He earned the trust shown when manager Ned Yost summoned him to relieve Young, two outs and one on against Josh Donaldson, one of the game's top sluggers. Hochevar threw a cutter at the letters, which Donaldson popped up, an easy out for Eric Hosmer that killed the Blue Jays' threat. After Hochevar came back the next inning for three more outs, he had gone through the Blue Jays' best four hitters in what has often been the Royals' vague and dangerous space between their rotation and top three relievers.

At one point, Hochevar was seen as the busted No. 1 pick, a sign of a sorry franchise's failures. Now he is remade into a valuable piece, equal parts talent and determination, a beloved teammate in the middle of the Royals' sprint toward another World Series.

Kansas City Royals center fielder Lorenzo Cain was safe at home despite the protest of Toronto Blue Jays starting pitcher R.A. Dickey after Cain scored on a wild pitch in the first inning.

Facing the heart of the Blue Jays batting order, Luke Hochevar worked 1⅓ innings and picked up his first postseason victory in relief of starter Chris Young.

Second baseman Ryan Goins still had his glove on Alex Rios when Rios' feet came off the bag on an attempted steal in the fourth. A review of the play determined Rios was out.

Story of the game

BY PETE GRATHOFF

1 Fantastic four
Alcides Escobar did his usual thing. He swung at the first pitch but missed. Then he bunted for a hit. Ben Zobrist then crushed a two-run homer. Lorenzo Cain walked, stole second and took third on Eric Hosmer's single. Another wild pitch allowed Cain to score as Hosmer took second. Kendrys Morales' ground-out got Hosmer to third and he scored on Mike Moustakas' long fly to center. Just like that it was 4-0. Chris Young struck out three and walked one in the the Toronto half.

4-0
KC-TOR

2 Rios hits a homer
Alex Rios blasted a one-out home run as Toronto starter R.A. Dickey continued to struggle. Escobar was hit by a pitch and moved to second on Zobrist's ground-out. After Cain walked, Dickey was yanked in favor of Liam Hendriks, who picked off Escobar. Young set Toronto down in order.

5-0
KC-TOR

3 Blue Jays on the board
After the Royals were set down in order, Toronto put together a rally. With one out, Ryan Goins singled and Ben Revere walked. Josh Donaldson lined a double that bounced over the left-field wall and Ryan Goins scored. Jose Bautista's ground-out to Zobrist got Revere home. But Young avoided further damage as Edwin Encarnacion flied to left.

5-2
KC-TOR

4 No love for replay
With two outs, Rios singled and was called safe on a steal of second. The Blue Jays challenged, and super-slow motion did show that Rios' foot came off the bag. His steal was wiped away. Toronto did nothing against Young.

5-2
KC-TOR

5 No news is good news
For the first time, the Royals went down in order. Revere singled with two outs, and manager Ned Yost called on Luke Hochevar to face Donaldson. The move paid off as Donaldson popped out.

5-2
KC-TOR

6 Force is with Luke Hochevar
It was three up and three down for the Royals again. More important, the same was true for the Blue Jays. For Hochevar, it was four batters faced and four retired.

5-2
KC-TOR

7 Another four-spot
Reliever LaTroy Hawkins entered for the Blue Jays and didn't get anyone out. Salvador Perez walked, and Alex Gordon and Rios singled. That loaded the bases, and Ryan Tepera was summoned. Escobar hit a deep fly to center that allowed each runner to move up a base, including Paulo Orlando, who was running for Rios. A wild pitch scored Gordon ahead of a Zobrist walk. Cain singled home a run, and Hosmer's fly to right scored Zobrist. All told, it was another four-run inning. Ryan Madson pitched a scoreless inning after giving up a leadoff single. That led to a great defensive play, as Madson snared a comebacker and threw to second, where Escobar made a diving grab of the off-target throw for a force-out.

9-2
KC-TOR

8 The fun continues
With one out, Perez doubled, Gordon walked, and Orlando singled as the bases were loaded again. Escobar hit a deep sacrifice fly, and Gordon scored on a wild pitch. Zobrist and Cain then singled, with the latter bringing home Orlando. That led to an exodus of Blue Jays fans.

12-2
KC-TOR

9 Blue Jays wave white flag
The offensive onslaught continued as Kendrys Morales singled. Two outs later, Gordon was hit by a pitch, and backup infielder Cliff Pennington was brought in to pitch. Orlando's single loaded the bases, and Escobar's single drove in two runs.

14-2
KC-TOR

ROYALS 14, BLUE JAYS 2

Kansas City	AB	R	H	BI	BB	SO	Avg.
A.Escobar ss	3	1	2	4	0	0	.600
Zobrist 2b	5	2	2	2	1	0	.389
L.Cain cf	3	1	2	3	2	1	.357
J.Dyson cf	0	0	0	0	0	0	---
Hosmer 1b	4	1	1	1	0	2	.313
K.Morales dh	5	1	1	0	0	0	.333
Moustakas 3b	4	0	0	1	0	1	.176
S.Perez c	3	2	1	0	1	1	.133
Butera c	1	0	0	0	0	0	.000
A.Gordon lf	3	3	1	0	1	0	.308
Rios rf	3	1	3	1	0	0	.308
1-Orlando pr-rf	2	2	2	0	0	0	1.000
Totals	36	14	15	12	5	5	

Toronto	AB	R	H	BI	BB	SO	Avg.
Revere lf	3	1	2	0	1	1	.188
Donaldson 3b	3	0	1	1	1	0	.333
Bautista rf	4	0	1	1	0	2	.167
Encarnacion dh	4	0	0	0	0	1	.250
Colabello 1b	4	0	0	0	0	1	.200
Tulowitzki ss	3	0	1	0	0	1	.333
a-Pompey ph	1	0	1	0	0	0	1.000
Ru.Martin c	3	0	0	0	0	1	.000
b-Carrera ph	1	0	0	0	0	0	.000
Pillar cf	4	0	0	0	0	2	.200
Goins 2b	3	1	1	0	0	1	.385
Totals	33	2	7	2	2	8	

Kansas City	410	000	432	—	14	15	0
Toronto	002	000	000	—	2	7	0

a-singled for Tulowitzki in the 9th. b-grounded out for Ru.Martin in the 9th. 1-ran for Rios in the 7th.
LOB: Kansas City 6, Toronto 6. **2B:** S.Perez (1), Donaldson (1). **HR:** Zobrist (1), off Dickey; Rios (1), off Dickey. **RBIs:** A.Escobar 4 (5), Zobrist 2 (3), L.Cain 3 (5), Hosmer (5), Moustakas (4), Rios (2), Donaldson (4), Bautista (2). **SB:** L.Cain (2), Donaldson (1). **CS:** Rios (1). **SF:** A.Escobar 2, Hosmer, Moustakas.
Runners left in scoring position: Kansas City 2 (Hosmer, Zobrist); Toronto 4 (Encarnacion 3, Pillar). **RISP:** Kansas City 8 for 11; Toronto 1 for 6. **Runners moved up:** Zobrist, K.Morales, Butera, Bautista, Carrera. **GIDP:** Encarnacion. **DP:** Kansas City 1 (A.Escobar, Zobrist, Hosmer).

Kansas City	IP	H	R	ER	BB	SO	NP	ERA
C.Young	4⅔	3	2	2	4	7	8	3.86
Hochevar W, 1-0	1⅓	1	0	0	0	0	12	0.00
Madson	1	1	0	0	0	2	15	0.00
K.Herrera	1	1	0	0	1	1	11	0.00
F.Morales	1	1	0	0	1	1	14	4.50

Toronto	IP	H	R	ER	BB	SO	NP	ERA
Dickey L, 0-1	1⅔	4	5	4	2	1	48	21.60
Hendriks	4⅓	1	0	0	0	2	59	5.79
Hawkins	0	2	3	3	1	0	11	45.00
Tepera	1⅔	5	4	4	2	0	38	21.60
Lowe	1	1	2	2	0	2	29	5.40
Pennington	⅓	2	0	0	0	0	7	0.00

Hawkins pitched to 3 batters in the 7th.
Inherited runners-scored: Hochevar 1-0, Hendriks 2-0, Tepera 3-3, Lowe 2-0, Pennington 2-2. **HBP:** by Dickey (A.Escobar), by Lowe (A.Gordon). **WP:** Tepera. **PB:** Ru.Martin.
Umpires: Home, Hunter Wendelstedt; First, Dan Iassogna; Second, Jeff Nelson; Third, Jim Reynolds; Left, Laz Diaz; Right, John Hirschbeck. **Time:** 3:39. **Att:** 49,501.

Royals shortstop Alcides Escobar (right) came up with an errant throw from pitcher Ryan Madson and forced out Toronto baserunner Troy Tulowitzki during the seventh inning.

Royals left fielder Alex Gordon (center) held his hand out for Ben Zobrist to slap after Gordon scored on a wild pitch in the seventh inning. Blue Jays catcher Russell Martin (left) had apparently seen too many Royals cross the plate by that time.

Pitcher Kelvin Herrera (right), brought in with the bases loaded, could only shake his head as Edwin Encarnacion and Jose Bautista scored on Troy Tulowitzki's double in the sixth.

JILL TOYOSHIBA

ALCS GAME 5

	123	456	789	R	H	E
Kansas City	000	000	010 —	1	4	0
Toronto	010	004	11x —	7	8	0

W W L W L 6 7

THE KANSAS CITY STAR

10/22/015

Party is put on ice

Blue Jays keep Royals from celebrating on their turf with 7-1 victory

Toronto breaks through against Volquez with four runs in the sixth

BY ANDY McCULLOUGH

TORONTO

On the ground floor of the Rogers Centre, Royals clubhouse attendants lugged bags of gear toward a waiting mover's truck. Somewhere in the luggage resided the cases of beer and champagne the team intended to spray in celebration of their second consecutive American League pennant. Instead, the suds - and the team - returned to the States after the Royals dropped a 7-1 decision to the Blue Jays in Game 5 of the American League Championship Series.

Instead of a coronation, the Royals opened a window for Toronto to swipe this series. A day after bludgeoning their hosts for 14 runs, the Royals fell under the spell of Toronto pitcher Marco Estrada. Edinson Volquez failed to repeat his traverse of the sixth-inning tightrope, the territory he covered in Game 1. Kelvin Herrera allowed Troy Tulowitzki to break the game open with a three-run double in the sixth, with all runs charged to Volquez.

"I think we're all right - we're up, 3-2, still, and we're going back to The K," third baseman Mike Moustakas said. "We didn't let anything slide by today. They earned that 'W.' They played well, they pitched well, they hit well. Didn't let anything slide by. They just beat us today."

Inside the clubhouse after the game, the dominant topic of conversation was the umpiring of Dan Iassogna behind the plate. He kept a tight strike zone as Volquez waded into trouble in the sixth inning.

Volquez said Iassogna apologized to catcher Salvador Perez for calling a full-count curveball to José Bautista a ball, though Perez later indicated this conversation did not occur. The walk loaded the bases and led to Tulowitzki's breakout hit.

Still, the Royals failed to generate any sort of offense against Estrada. He faced one over the minimum through seven innings. The solo blemish on his line was a homer struck by Perez in the eighth.

"He was executing his pitches pretty much from the beginning," first baseman Eric Hosmer said. "He threw a good game. We just couldn't get anything going offensively."

In defeat, the Royals acknowledged the might of their opponents. The Blue Jays wielded baseball's best offense in the regular season. Even after Tuesday's thrashing, manager Ned Yost insisted the task of clinching in Canada was tall.

"After winning the first two games, in reality your goal is to come to Toronto - kind of a foreign environment, a hostile environment, and at least win one," Yost said. "Then you get to go home and win one there and the series is over."

During the regular season, Volquez hummed a fastball clocked at a 93.7 mph average, according to FanGraphs. He fired heaters that reached 98 mph in the first inning Wednesday.

Volquez ran into trouble against the fifth batter he faced. With the count 0-2 to first baseman Chris Colabello, Volquez left a change-up over the middle of the plate. Colabello woke up the park with a solo homer to left.

"I'm going to call him my daddy," Volquez said. "He's got my number."

As part of this Game 1 rematch, Toronto used Estrada on the mound. Manager John Gibbons was desperate for a lengthy outing from Estrada.

The first Kansas City hit did not occur until Alcides Escobar singled to open the fourth. He was promptly erased when Ben Zobrist hit into a double play.

The Royals still trailed by one when the bottom of the sixth

JOHN SLEEZER

Royals third baseman Mike Moustakas threw his helmet off and walked away from home plate after striking out in the second inning.

began. Volquez issued a leadoff walk to Ben Revere and hit Josh Donaldson with a fastball on the elbow pad.

"I started walking people," Volquez said. "You can't do that in a big game."

Up came Bautista for an encounter that heightened Kansas City's tension with the umpire. Volquez could not find a strike on the outer half of the plate, and Bautista went ahead 3-1 in the count. Bautista fouled back five consecutive fastballs, all of them clocked at 96 mph or faster.

At last Perez called for the first off-speed pitch of the at-bat. Volquez spun a curve that broke at the thighs, bound for the far-most edge of the plate. Bautista caught himself in midswing.

Volquez and Perez thought the pitch was a strike. Yost thought Bautista might have swung. But Yost could not communicate with the umpires to request an appeal to the first-base umpire.

"I couldn't get anybody's attention because the crowd was so loud," Yost said. "If those things linger, you're never going to get the call."

To reporters inside the home clubhouse, Bautista acknowledged his good fortune.

"You could argue I got the benefit of a borderline call," he said.

In the infield, Escobar and Zobrist raged at the walk. Their ire would only increase. Again Volquez tried to spot backdoor, two-seam sinkers, this time to Edwin Encarnacion. Again Volquez missed, in the eye of Iassogna, but close enough to irritate the Royals. When Encarnacion drove in a run on Volquez's third walk of the inning, Escobar pointed toward the umpire and hollered.

"From shortstop, for me, that's a strike," Escobar said. "I don't know. I didn't see the replay yet. But those were really close pitches."

Yost argued with Iassogna after he removed Volquez and inserted Herrera. Yost returned to the dugout and watched Tulowitzki bash a 99-mph, first-pitch fastball and clear the bases.

An inning later, Danny Duffy yielded an RBI double to Bautista. Another RBI double by Kevin Pillar in the eighth swelled Toronto's advantage.

Now a seven-game series is reduced to two. If Kansas City can win once, they'll claim another pennant. If they allow Toronto to steal this series from them, they'll rue missed chances at the Rogers Centre. Game 6 happens Friday night at Kauffman Stadium.

"That's the best way to end it," Volquez said. "In Kansas City. That's where we live. It's where we play. It's always a great feeling to be back in Kansas City."

SHANE KEYSER

Royals center fielder Lorenzo Cain couldn't catch an RBI double by Toronto's Kevin Pillar in the eighth inning.

Story of the game

BY PETE GRATHOFF

1 No fast start

A day after putting a four-spot on the board in the first inning, the Royals went down in order against Marco Estrada, proving that Alcides Escobar can indeed make an out when leading off a game. Edinson Volquez looked sharp, too, as the Blue Jays didn't hit the ball out of the infield.

0-0
KC-TOR

2 Toronto takes the lead

The Royals were set down in order again, but the Blue Jays grabbed the lead on Chris Colabello's solo home run to left-center field with one out. Troy Tulowitzki lined to third baseman Mike Moustakas, and Dioner Navarro drew a walk. But Volquez avoided more trouble when Kevin Pillar lined out to second baseman Ben Zobrist.

1-0
TOR-KC

3 Nothing to see here

It was another three-up and three-down inning for Estrada, though Salvador Perez did line out sharply to Tulowitzki at short. Volquez got three ground-outs and the score didn't change.

1-0
TOR-KC

4 Double play, double play

With one swing, Escobar broke up the perfect game with a single to left field. However, Zobrist followed by hitting into a 4-6-3 double play. Jose Bautista opened the inning with an infield single, despite a nice play by Escobar. Edwin Encarnacion's ground-out forced Bautista at second and Colabello followed by hitting into a 6-4-3 double play.

1-0
TOR-KC

5 Still a one-run game

The Royals' bats remained quiet as Estrada set them down in order again. Volquez allowed a two-out single to Pillar, but Ryan Goins grounded out to Eric Hosmer at first base.

1-0
TOR-KC

6 A great gnashing of teeth

The Royals hit two balls to the outfield, which constituted a rally at this point. Volquez didn't get an out in his half of the inning. Ben Revere walked and Josh Donaldson was hit by a pitch. Volquez and Bautista engaged in a great 10-pitch battle. A couple of close pitches didn't go Volquez's way and Bautista walked, loading the bases. Volquez then walked Encarnacion, forcing in a run. While replacing Volquez with Kelvin Herrera, Ned Yost had a few choice words with home-plate umpire Dan Iassogna. Herrera struck out Colabello, but Tulowitzki hit a bases-clearing double.

5-0
TOR-KC

7 There's another run

The beat went on in the seventh. Cain drew a two-out walk, but it didn't start a rally because Hosmer flied to left and ended the inning. Reliever Danny Duffy took over for the Royals and got two strike-outs. Then he gave up doubles to Donaldson and Bautista, and the Blue Jays exended their lead.

6-0
TOR-KC

8 Finally, some good news

The Royals got on the board as Perez hit an opposite-field home run. Alex Gordon followed with a single, and there was a glimmer of hope. Aaron Sanchez took over for Estrada, and Alex Rios greeted him with a single. But the rally ended when Escobar flied to right. Toronto got the run back as Tulowitzki singled with one out. After another out, Pillar doubled home Tulowitzki.

7-1
TOR-KC

9 Coming home

Roberto Osuna took over in the ninth for the Blue Jays and got three ground-outs as the Blue Jays stayed alive in the series.

7-1
TOR-KC

BLUE JAYS 7, ROYALS 1

Kansas City	AB	R	H	BI	BB	SO	Avg.
A.Escobar ss	4	0	1	0	0	0	.526
Zobrist 2b	4	0	0	0	0	1	.318
L.Cain cf	3	0	0	0	1	1	.294
Hosmer 1b	4	0	0	0	0	0	.250
K.Morales dh	3	0	0	0	0	1	.278
Moustakas 3b	3	0	0	0	0	1	.150
S.Perez c	3	1	1	1	0	0	.167
A.Gordon lf	3	0	1	0	0	1	.313
Rios rf	3	0	1	0	0	0	.313
Totals	30	1	4	1	1	5	

Toronto	AB	R	H	BI	BB	SO	Avg.
Revere lf	3	1	0	0	1	1	.158
Donaldson 3b	3	2	1	0	0	1	.333
Bautista rf	3	1	2	1	1	0	.267
Encarnacion dh	3	1	0	1	1	1	.211
Colabello 1b	4	1	1	1	0	2	.211
Smoak 1b	0	0	0	0	0	0	.000
Tulowitzki ss	4	1	2	3	0	0	.368
D.Navarro c	3	0	0	0	1	3	.000
Pillar cf	4	0	2	1	0	1	.263
Goins 2b	3	0	0	0	0	1	.313
Totals	30	7	8	7	4	10	

Kansas City	000	000	010	—	1	4	0
Toronto	010	004	11x	—	7	8	0

LOB: Kansas City 3, Toronto 4. **2B:** Donaldson (2), Bautista (1), Tulowitzki (2), Pillar (3). **HR:** S.Perez (2), off Estrada; Colabello (1), off Volquez. **RBIs:** S.Perez (2), Bautista (3), Encarnacion (3), Colabello (1), Tulowitzki 3 (7), Pillar (2).
Runners left in scoring position: Kansas City 1 (A.Escobar); Toronto 2 (Pillar, Encarnacion). **RISP:** Kansas City 0 for 1; Toronto 2 for 6. **GIDP:** Zobrist, Colabello. **DP:** Kansas City 1 (Zobrist, A.Escobar, Hosmer); Toronto 1 (Goins, Tulowitzki, Colabello).

Kansas City	IP	H	R	ER	BB	SO	NP	ERA
Volquez L, 1-1	5	3	5	5	4	2	88	4.09
K.Herrera	1	1	0	0	0	3	13	0.00
D.Duffy	2	4	2	2	0	5	32	6.00

Toronto	IP	H	R	ER	BB	SO	NP	ERA
Estrada W, 1-1	7⅔	3	1	1	1	5	108	2.77
Aa.Sanchez	⅓	1	0	0	0	0	8	0.00
Osuna	1	0	0	0	0	5	5	5.40

Volquez pitched to 4 batters in the 6th.
Inherited runners-scored: K.Herrera 3-3, Aa.Sanchez 1-0. **HBP:** by Volquez (Donaldson).
Umpires: Home, Dan Iassogna; First, Jeff Nelson; Second, Jim Reynolds; Third, Laz Diaz; Left, John Hirschbeck; Right, Hunter Wendelstedt. **Time:** 2:56. **Att:** 49,325.

The Blue Jays successfully challenged the call that Mike Moustakas tagged Kevin Pillar, who tried to stretch a double into a triple Wednesday. Earlier in the playoffs, two Royals base runners were called out on challenges after sliding.

Shortstop Alcides Escobar forced Toronto Blue Jays designated hitter Edwin Encarnacion out at second and turned the double play in the fourth.

Left fielder Alex Gordon flipped his bat after striking out in the third inning.

Replay on players' slides spurs talk

The Royals on Tuesday lost a second runner on a stolen base to a replay challenge in the postseason

TORONTO
The replay call that went against the Royals on Tuesday in Game 4 of the American League Championship Series, when Alex Rios came off the bag on a stolen-base attempt, had Royals fans grumbling and some asking if such calls were in the spirit of replay.

To reset: With two outs in the fourth inning and the Royals leading 5-2, Rios singled and took off for second on the first pitch to the next batter, Alcides Escobar.

Rios and the throw from Blue Jays catcher Russell Martin arrived about the same time, but the throw was high. Rios had the base stolen, until he popped up on his feet-first slide and both feet came off the base. Jays second baseman Ryan Goins kept the tag on Rios and the replay clearly showed Rios had come off the bag. The call was overturned. Rios was out.

Some have argued that replay wasn't intended for such plays and runs contrary to the spirit of the expanded system that was put in place in 2014. Whether a ball was fair or foul or a ball was trapped or caught. Not whether a base stealer's momentum forced him to lose contact with the bag for a fraction of a second.

"But that's the way the game is," Royals manager Ned Yost said Wednesday before Game 5. "The technology is so good right now you see things evolve … like before last year infielders wouldn't hold the tag on the runner. They'd just tag and get off.

"Now because of instant replay, you see everybody holding the tag on the runner."

- Blair Kerkhoff

JOHN SLEEZER

A throw from Kansas City Royals shortstop Alcides Escobar got past the glove of first baseman Eric Hosmer as Toronto Blue Jays right fielder Jose Bautista slid into first on a single in the fourth inning.

SHANE KEYSER

Blue Jays shortstop Troy Tulowitzki connected for a three-run double against Royals reliever Kelvin Herrera that broke Game 5 open in the sixth inning.

Kansas City Royals players celebrated winning the ALCS championship over Toronto 4-3 at Kauffman Stadium.

JILL TOYOSHIBA

ALCS GAME 6

	123	456	789	R	H	E
Toronto	000	100	020 —	3	7	0
Kansas City	110	000	11x —	4	9	0

      (7)

THE KANSAS CITY STAR

10/24/015

Dash back to Series

....

Lorenzo Cain scores from first on a Eric Hosmer single to give Royals 4-3 win

....

Wade Davis puts two on, strikes out two and gets a ground-out in the ninth

....

——————

BY ANDY McCULLOUGH

The savior for Ned Yost, the right arm who waved the Kansas City Royals into their second World Series in a row, stood a few feet shy of third base as Eric Hosmer's single soared into right field. Mike Jirschele, a minor-league lifer turned big-league coach, squinted as the baseball settled into the corner.

He earned infamy among certain fans for his refusal to send Alex Gordon in Game 7 of the World Series last year. Now he transformed his arm into a windmill, ordering Lorenzo Cain homeward, bringing in the pennant-capturing run in the eighth inning of a 4-3 Royals victory over the Blue Jays in Game 6 of the American League Championship Series.

The RBI single from Eric Hosmer, who scored Cain all the way from first, capped a gut-wrenching evening with a scene of ecstasy. The Royals benefited from a mistake by outfielder Jose Bautista, who thundered two home runs on this night, but chose to throw to second rather than home on Hosmer's hit. Jirschele saw it all the way, and the Royals ran straight back into the World Series.

In the bottom of the inning, Wade Davis stared down Josh Donaldson, the probable American League MVP, with two outs and two on. Softened by the rain, wrenched into misalignment by Yost, Davis still induced a ground-out to send the Royals back to the Fall Classic.

Davis collected the save after sitting out more than an hour because of a rain delay in the eighth inning. He helped camouflage a colossal blunder by Yost before the rain came.

The eighth inning was a catastrophe wrought by inclement

SHANE KEYSER

Royals center fielder Lorenzo Cain celebrated scoring the go-ahead run on an RBI single in the eighth inning by first baseman Eric Hosmer.

weather and ill-advised bullpen usage. Holding a two-run lead heading into the eighth, Yost chose Ryan Madson to pitch instead of sending in Davis for a six-out save.

Two pitches into his outing, Davis started to warm up, creating a surreal split-screen that heightened the madness of the inning. Madson gave up an infield single to outfielder Ben Revere. He struck out Josh Donaldson. But facing Jose Bautista, Madson threw a 96-mph fastball at the letters.

As Davis threw to the bullpen catcher, the baseball soared in his direction. The sight shocked the crowd, packed to capacity and prepared to celebrate the pennant. After a walk to Edwin Encarnacion, Yost pulled Madson and sent in Davis, who promptly retired the next two batters.

At this point, the rain intervened. The game entered a delay that lasted 45 minutes. The weather may have played a role in Yost's thought process, as he did not want to lose Davis for the ninth inning due to the weather. Even so, he still chose to expose Madson to the best hitters on Toronto's lineup, rather than deploying Davis, an All-Star and perhaps the best reliever in the American League.

And yet the Royals still won. The offense is too talented. And Davis appears indomitable.

Ben Zobrist and Mike Moustakas supplied home runs in the first two innings against Toronto ace David Price, who stymied the Royals thereafter. At last the hitters chased him in the seventh. Alex Rios continued his torrid postseason with an RBI single off reliever Aaron Sanchez.

Yordano Ventura held Toronto to one run in 5⅓ innings. Kelvin Herrera collected the next five outs. Plenty of drama awaited around the corner.

Fighting to stave off elimination, Toronto started Price, the southpaw star they acquired shortly before the trade deadline.

In the bottom of the first, Price spun a cutter toward Zobrist, his former teammate in Tampa Bay. Zobrist stung a drive down the left-field line. The ball just cleared the fence.

An inning later, Moustakas unloaded on a 1-2 change-up and scorched a line drive toward the Pepsi Porch in right-center field.

As the ball approached the stands, a pair of fans wearing gloves reached over the railing. The winner was Caleb Humphreys, a bearded, bespectacled 19-year-old from Blue Springs. Humphreys

Fan nearly interferes with critical home run

Play was reviewed after Blue Jays replay challenge but home run stood

With the Royals leading the Blue Jays 1-0 in the second inning, Mike Moustakas stepped to the plate and crushed a 1-2 change-up from David Price. The ball soared toward the top of the wall in right field. Caleb Humphreys, 19, could see it coming right toward him. As the baseball fell toward the top of the padding, Humphreys leaned forward and snagged the ball just inches from the top of the wall. On the field, the umpire initially signaled for a solo homer. But moments later, Blue Jays manager John Gibbons emerged to issue a challenge.

As he sat in his seat, Humphreys insisted that he did not reach into the field of play or commit fan interference, which could have turned the homer into a ground-rule double. After an official review, the umpires concurred, saying they could not determine if Humphrey's first contact with the baseball came over the field of play.

After securing the catch, Humphreys saw Toronto outfielder Kevin Pillar running his way, pointing up toward his seat. When the replay began, he said, his stomach began to roil.

"When I saw the umpires get together, I got kind of worried," Humphreys said. "But after seeing it over here (on the scoreboard), I felt pretty safe."

As the game forged on, Humphreys peered back over the wall, the gap between the railing and the edge of the padding. He clutched his glove in his hands.

"I wasn't going to bring it," he said. "I usually sit over by the dugout, so I don't need it. With these seats, right before I left, I decided I better bring it.

"I don't know. I guess I just had a feeling I might need it."

- Rustin Dodd

caught the ball as the crowd went wild.

Down on the field, Bautista pointed in disgust. Toronto manager John Gibbons asked for a challenge. As the umpires conferenced with replay officials in New York, Humphreys felt nervous. He told a reporter from The Star he was praying for the homer to be upheld.

The prayer of Humphreys and thousands of others issued inside the park during the interim were answered. The homer stood. The lead doubled.

Up two, responsibility transferred to Ventura's slender shoulders. He had been wobbly for much of the postseason, with opposing hitters clubbing him to the tune of a .909 on-base-plus-slugging percentage. As a fix, he tried a subtle technical tweak.

Ventura operated exclusively out of the stretch from the start on Friday. Dividends were paid early on, as Ventura struck out four with his curveball in three scoreless innings.

In the fourth, he fell behind Bautista, 3-1. Sitting on the fastball, Bautista obliterated a drive that nearly reached the Royals Hall of Fame past the left-field fence.

The blast did not dent Ventura's confidence. He left shortstop Troy Tulowitzki motionless with a full-count curveball to end the inning.

Ventura lacked the polish of his first four innings. He walked catcher Russell Martin. After a walk to outfielder Kevin Pillar, the bullpen phone rang and Luke Hochevar stood up. Inside the dugout, Yost made no move toward the mound.

The lineup turned over when second baseman Ryan Goins flied out to center. A fly-out by leadoff hitter Ben Revere allowed Yost an opportunity to intervene. Surely he would send Hochevar to face Donaldson, Toronto's most dangerous hitter.

A gathering convened on the mound. Yost was not part of it.

Donaldson scalded a low line drive down the line. The ball's journey ended in the webbing of Moustakas' glove, ending the inning.

Despite the escape, Yost continued to tempt fate. He sent Ventura back out to face Bautista to start the sixth. Bautista hit a harmless fly, but Encarnacion thumped a two-base hit to the wall. The double ended Ventura's night and placed the fate of the Royals in the hands of their bullpen.

In first was Kelvin Herrera. He blew away first baseman Chris Colabello with a 100-mph fastball for one out. Two days after giving up a critical double to Tulowitzki, Herrera induced an inning-ended flyball in the rematch.

Herrera returned for the seventh and pitched a spotless inning. Now came the critical decision for Yost: Madson or Davis? He chose Madson. The decision backfired. But the Royals still survived.

Royals starting pitcher Yordano Ventura was fired up as he walked off the mound after pitching the top of the fourth inning.

Royals third baseman Mike Moustakas took off running after he hit a solo home run in the second inning.

Story of the game

BY PETE GRATHOFF

1 **Off to a good start**
Ben Revere opened the game with a double to right, but Yordano Ventura struck out Josh Donaldson, got Jose Bautista on a fly to right and Edwin Encarnacion grounded to third. With one out in the Royals' half, Ben Zobrist yanked a 1-1 offering from David Price over the left-field wall.

1-0
KC-TOR

2 **So far, so good**
Ventura looked sharp, setting down Toronto in order, punctuated by a called strikeout of Russell Martin. With one out, Mike Moustakas hit a laser to right-center field. The ball was grabbed just above the wall by a Royals fan. The Blue Jays had the umpires challenge, saying it was interference, but the homer stood.

2-0
KC-TOR

3 **Royals leave two on**
Kevin Pillar squared up a ball and lined it toward Eric Hosmer at first base. Hosmer made a nice leaping grab of the ball, and Ventura got a pair of strikeouts to end the inning. The Royals made some noise with two outs. Zobrist walked and Lorenzo Cain hit a squibber past the mound and reached on an infield single. Hosmer grounded to second to end the inning.

2-0
KC-TOR

4 **Lead is cut in half**
With one out, Bautista drew more boos when he crushed a 3-1 offering from Ventura deep to left. The ball was thrown back on the field, but the run, of course, counted. After another out, Chris Colabello singled, but Ventura struck out Troy Tulowitzki looking. Ventura took a few steps toward the plate and stared at Tulowitzki, but home-plate umpire Jeff Nelson encouraged Ventura to go to the dugout. Price struck out the side in the bottom of the inning.

2-1
KC-TOR

5 **Ventura escapes trouble**
Martin and Pillar drew leadoff walks, and that prompted Ned Yost to get Luke Hochevar up in the bullpen. Ryan Goins couldn't get a bunt down and flied to center, Revere flied to left and Josh Donaldson hit a laser that Moustakas dived and grabbed. Alex Rios singled with one out for the Royals, and stole second with two outs. But Zobrist popped out to second, ending the inning.

2-1
KC-TOR

6 **Herrera squelches threat**
Ventura returned for the sixth inning and got Bautista to fly to center before Encarnacion doubled. Kelvin Herrera entered and struck out Colabello and got Tulowitzki to fly to center. The Royals went down in order against Price.

2-1
KC-TOR

7 **An insurance run**
Herrera had little trouble making it through the inning. He got two fly-ball outs and struck out Goins. Moustakas opened with a bloop single to center for the Royals. Salvador Perez hit a fly to deep left that Revere made a great catch on as he hit the wall at the Royals' bullpen. Moustakas was nearly doubled off, but he moved to second on a grounder by Alex Gordon. Aaron Sanchez took over for Price, and Rios greeted him with a single to left that scored Moustakas.

3-1
KC-TOR

8 **Crazy eighth**
Ryan Madson opened the eighth for the Royals and allowed a single to Revere. Donaldson struck out looking, then Bautista silenced the 40,494 at Kauffman Stadium by hitting a home run to left field. Encarnacion walked, and Wade Davis came on and got two outs. Rain began falling and there was a 45-minute delay. The Blue Jays brought on closer Roberto Osuna. Cain drew a leadoff walk and Hosmer singled to right field. Bautista had to run to get to the ball, then inexplicably threw to second base. Hosmer retreated to first, but Cain never stopped running and scored the go-ahead run.

4-3
KC-TOR

9 **Never in doubt, right?**
After sitting for about an hour, Davis returned, and Martin hit a bloop single. Pinch runner Dalton Pompey stole second and third, and Pillar walked. Dioner Navarro hit for Goins and struck out as Pillar stole second. Revere then struck out, and Donaldson grounded to Moustakas.

4-3
KC-TOR

ROYALS 4, BLUE JAYS 3

Toronto	AB	R	H	BI	BB	SO	Avg.
Revere lf	5	1	2	0	0	2	.208
Donaldson 3b	5	0	0	0	0	2	.261
Bautista rf	4	2	2	3	0	0	.316
Encarnacion dh	3	0	1	0	1	0	.227
Colabello 1b	4	0	1	0	0	1	.217
Tulowitzki ss	4	0	0	0	0	2	.304
Ru.Martin c	3	0	1	0	1	1	.091
3-Pompey pr	0	0	0	0	0	0	1.000
Pillar cf	2	0	0	0	2	0	.238
Goins 2b	3	0	0	0	0	2	.263
a-D.Navarro ph	1	0	0	0	0	1	.000
Totals	**34**	**3**	**7**	**3**	**4**	**11**	

Kansas City	AB	R	H	BI	BB	SO	Avg.
A.Escobar ss	4	0	1	0	0	1	.478
Zobrist 2b	3	1	1	1	1	0	.320
L.Cain cf	3	1	1	0	1	0	.300
Hosmer 1b	4	0	1	1	0	1	.250
K.Morales dh	4	0	1	0	0	1	.273
2-Gore pr-dh	0	0	0	0	0	0	---
Moustakas 3b	4	2	2	1	0	1	.208
S.Perez c	4	0	0	0	0	2	.136
A.Gordon lf	3	0	0	0	2	0	.263
Rios rf	3	0	2	1	0	0	.368
1-Orlando pr-rf	0	0	0	0	0	0	1.000
Totals	**32**	**4**	**9**	**4**	**2**	**8**	

Toronto	000	100	020	—	3	7	0
Kansas City	110	000	11x	—	4	9	0

a-struck out for Goins in the 9th.
1-ran for Rios in the 7th. 2-ran for K.Morales in the 8th. 3-ran for Ru.Martin in the 9th.

LOB: Toronto 8, Kansas City 6. **2B:** Revere (1), Encarnacion (1). **HR:** Bautista (1), off Ventura; Bautista (2), off Madson; Zobrist (2), off Price; Moustakas (1), off Price. **RBIs:** Bautista 3 (6), Zobrist (4), Hosmer (6), Moustakas (5), Rios (3). **SB:** Pompey 2 (2), Pillar (2), Rios (1).
Runners left in scoring position: Toronto 6 (Encarnacion, Donaldson 3, Tulowitzki 2); Kansas City 4 (Hosmer, Zobrist 2, S.Perez). **RISP:** Toronto 0 for 12; Kansas City 1 for 6. **Runners moved up:** A.Gordon. **GIDP:** S.Perez. **DP:** Toronto 1 (Tulowitzki, Goins, Colabello).

Toronto	IP	H	R	ER	BB	SO	NP	ERA
Price	6⅔	5	3	3	1	8	99	5.40
Aa.Sanchez	⅓	2	0	0	0	0	6	0.00
Osuna L, 0-1	1	2	1	1	1	0	23	6.75

Kansas City	IP	H	R	ER	BB	SO	NP	ERA
Ventura	5⅓	4	1	1	2	5	77	3.38
K.Herrera	1⅔	0	0	0	0	2	21	0.00
Madson	⅓	2	2	2	1	1	16	7.71
W.Davis W, 1-0	1⅔	1	0	0	1	3	30	0.00

Blown save: Madson (1). **Holds:** K.Herrera (3). **Inherited runners-scored:** Aa.Sanchez 1-1, K.Herrera 1-0, W.Davis 1-0. **WP:** W.Davis.
Umpires: Home, Jeff Nelson; First, Jim Reynolds; Second, Laz Diaz; Third, John Hirschbeck; Left, Hunter Wendelstedt; Right, Dan Iassogna. **Time:** 3:22 (Delay: 0:45). **Att:** 40,494.

SHANE KEYSER

Shortstop Alcides Escobar hoisted the ALCS MVP trophy while holding one of his children after the Royals won the ALCS championship.

JOHN SLEEZER

Wade Davis got the final out of the ninth inning and gave the Royals an American League pennant.

JOHN SLEEZER

Mike Moustakas celebrated with teammates after their 4-3 win over the Toronto Blue Jays.

Fans in the stands

ALLISON LONG

'Miss Frances' has won over hearts at The K

They know Frances Ingemann well at Kauffman Stadium. The 88-year-old has held season tickets since 1985. She drives in alone from Lawrence, and didn't get home until 2 a.m. Wednesday but was back for more that night for Game 2.

The ushers know her as "Miss Frances," a fervent fan of slight build who declines their help when she ascends the steps.

She enjoys one beer every game, a Boulevard wheat.

And she knows her baseball.

Wednesday night during the third inning, Ingemann pointed to starting pitcher Johnny Cueto's statistics displayed above left field.

"Look at that balls-to-strikes ratio. Ten to 22. Pretty good," she said.

- Rick Montgomery

Royals honor the memory of young fan

Scott Wilson talked to his daughter, Natalie Wilson, as he sat in the Buck O'Neil Legacy Seat in honor of his late son, Noah, on Wednesday at Kauffman Stadium.

Had things been different, Noah Wilson would have celebrated his eighth birthday Wednesday.

He'd probably be at the World Series rooting on his Royals.

But even though Noah's brave battle with cancer ended in his death June 30 at Children's Mercy Hospital, the Royals made sure he had a seat for Game 2.

Noah was 6 when he was diagnosed with Ewing's sarcoma, a rare bone cancer that put him through an intense regimen of chemotherapy and radiation treatments.

The Royals, particularly first baseman Eric Hosmer, last year brought Noah under the team's wing. The club helped promote the Bandage Project, a charity that Noah launched as a cancer patient to provide colorful bandages to hospitalized kids.

- Rick Montgomery

ALLISON LONG

Newlyweds tie knot, go to game

Tricia Freeman's wedding day started out conventionally enough.

At about 1 p.m. Saturday, Freeman walked down the aisle toward her soon-to-be husband, Kyle Kovach.

Three hours later, the newlyweds walked down the steps of a party bus and through Gate D of Kauffman Stadium for Game 2 of the American League Championship Series.

"At first, I was like 'We can't go, because we have a wedding to go to, and that's ours,' " Kyle said.

But with a little finagling, the couple was able to squeeze in a few innings before their 6:30 reception in downtown Kansas City.

"I grew up watching the Royals," Tricia said. "My family, we all love the Royals and we just cannot imagine anything better than this."

- Melissa Graham

MELISSA GRAHAM

Faces in the crowd

Royals fans aren't afraid to go all out to express their love of the team. Here's a few of our favorite shots.

JILL TOYOSHIBA

JILL TOYOSHIBA

JILL TOYOSHIBA

JILL TOYOSHIBA

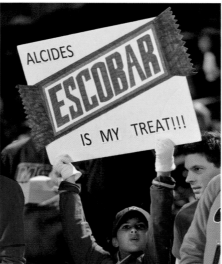

JOHN SLEEZER

JOHN SLEEZER

Encore!

Royals left fielder Alex Gordon rounded first after hitting the game-tying home run off Jeurys Familia in the ninth inning of Game 1 of the World Series.

ALLISON LONG

WORLD SERIES GAME 1

	1 2 3 4 5 6 7 8 9 10 11 12 13 14	R	H	E
New York	000 111 010 000 00	4	11	1
Kansas City	100 002 001 000 01	5	11	1

   W 2 3 4 5 6 7

THE KANSAS CITY STAR

10/28/15

Midnight special

....

Eric Hosmer's bases-loaded sacrifice fly in bottom of 14th scores Alcides Escobar

....

Game goes to extra innings as Alex Gordon's homer with one out in bottom of ninth ties game 4-4

....

Escobar hits Harvey's first pitch for inside-the-park homer

....

———

BY ANDY McCULLOUGH

He strode to the plate at 15 minutes past midnight, six innings and a calendar day removed from exiting this ballpark looking like a goat. Eric Hosmer came to the plate with the bases fully stocked with Royals and none out in the 14th inning of Game 1 of the World Series. He did not have to do too much. He did not try.

Hosmer lifted a sacrifice fly to right field, deep enough to plate Alcides Escobar, the winning blow after five hours and nine minutes of gut-wrenching baseball in a 5-4 victory over the Mets.

The Mets left 11 runners on base; the Royals countered with 11 of their own. The Kansas City relievers allowed one run across eight innings and struck out 12. The victory belonged to Chris Young, the team's Game 4 starter, who contributed three innings of emergency relief.

And to think it all appeared over when the ninth inning began.

JOHN SLEEZER

Royals second baseman Ben Zobrist celebrated with first baseman Eric Hosmer after Hosmer drove Zobrist home with a sacrifice fly in the sixth inning during Game 1 of the World Series.

Two outs away from defeat, Alex Gordon unloaded a titanic blast over the center-field fence off Mets closer Jeurys Familia. Familia had not blown a save in three months. The baseball traveled an estimated 428 feet and awakened a sullen stadium. In the dugout, Hosmer found Gordon and gave him a hug. Gordon removed some guilt from Hosmer's conscience.

New York grabbed the lead with the mirror image of their final flourish against the Red Sox in Game 6 of that World Series. The grounder that conquered Hosmer represented a far greater challenge than the one that rolled between Bill Buckner's legs. But still it stung.

The ball chopped off the bat of shortstop Wilmer Flores. Ready to run at second was mid-game entrant Juan Lagares, who had singled off Kelvin Herrera and stolen second. Now he jetted home after the ball skipped by Hosmer.

Edinson Volquez turned in the minimum requirement of a quality start, with three runs allowed across six innings. He still matched the output of Mets starter Matt Harvey, who the Royals toppled with a two-run rally in the sixth. Shortly after Ben Zobrist doubled and scored, Mike Moustakas tied the game with an RBI single to plate Cain.

Oddities marked the early portion of the game. Escobar smashed the first pitch he saw for an inside-the-park homer in the first. The Fox broadcast went out in the fourth, which forced both teams to play without replay reviews for a stretch. A misty drizzle covered the park.

The clouds cleared, relatively, in time for the game to begin without delay. As Volquez took the mound, reports proliferated on social media about the death of his father in the Dominican Republic.

The reports emerged as Volquez loosened up in the bullpen about 30 minutes before the first pitch. It was unclear if the news had reached Volquez.

After Volquez vanquished the first three hitters he faced, Escobar handed him a one-run lead. Escobar came to the plate for his first at-bat since winning the American League Championship Series MVP. He hit .478 against Toronto, and swung at the first pitch in the first inning in all six games. At one point, he admitted he hacked so often in those spots because 99 percent of the time, the opposing pitcher threw a fastball for a strike.

Either Harvey ignored the scouting report or he refused to bend to Escobar's tendencies. Harvey heaved a 95-mph fastball over the plate. True to form, Escobar swung.

Escobar cracked the baseball into the left-center gap, closer to Yoenis Cespedes than rookie left fielder Michael Conforto.

The duo converged but struggled to communicate. At the last moment, Cespedes opened his glove for a half-hearted, hopeless stab. The baseball fell to earth and rattled along the warning track.

Escobar never stopped running. He spotted the green light from third-base coach Mike Jirschele. Escobar did not even need to slide.

Daniel Murphy, the Mets' postseason version of Babe Ruth, led off the fourth with a single up the middle. Lucas Duda chopped a single up the middle. Moustakas dived to smother a grounder off the bat of catcher Travis d'Arnaud, but could not make a play on the RBI infield single.

The game veered off the path in the bottom of the fourth. After Harvey fanned Kendrys Morales, Mets manager Terry Collins emerged from his dugout to speak with umpire Bill Welke. Welke left to speak with Ned Yost. The Fox truck at the ballpark lost power, which cut out the video feeds inside the clubhouses, robbing both teams of replay capabilities.

The delay lasted about five minutes. Both teams reacquired replay in the top of the fifth, using an international feed from MLB. This left the Royals with the renewed ability to re-watch Curtis Granderson's go-ahead homer in the fifth.

Volquez led in the count, 1-2, when he fired a 95-mph sinker. The pitch bisected the plate. Granderson made it disappear inside the Mets bullpen in right field.

An inning later, the Mets continued to harass Volquez. Yoenis Cespedes led off with a single. Duda grounded a single up the middle, where the Royals presented an infield shift. Moustakas stood along on the first-base side of second. He had to range to his left, toward first, to corral Duda's grounder. He could not handle it, and Cespedes rumbled to third.

Two batters later, Conforto lifted a fly ball to left field. Alex Gordon settled underneath. As soon as Gordon caught the ball, Cespedes sprinted home. The throw was not close, and the Mets led by two.

Zobrist did not allow his teammates to hang their heads for long. He stroked Harvey's first pitch in the bottom of the frame, a 94-mph fastball, into the right-field corner for a double. Lorenzo Cain shot a single into right. With runners at the corners, Hosmer managed a run-scoring fly ball to center.

The inning created a microcosm of Kansas City baseball. Harvey occupied himself with the task of keeping Cain at first. He threw to first four times as he faced Hosmer and Kendrys Morales. And still Cain swiped the bag. The stolen base also protected against a double play, because Morales grounded back to Harvey for the second out.

Moustakas passed on a pair of curveballs to start his encounter with Harvey. He did not ignore the subsequent change-up, even though it dived toward the opposing batter's box. Moustakas ripped the pitch into right-center to score Cain.

Yet two innings later, in a similar situation, the Royals shifted away from their strengths. Cain could not put down the bunt. Kansas City could not even the game.

Until the ninth, when Gordon homered.

ALLISON LONG

Hall of Famer George Brett threw out the ceremonial first pitch at Kauffman Stadium for Game 1 of the World Series. Mike Moustakas was his catcher.

JOHN SLEEZER

Starting pitcher Edinson Volquez pumped his fist after striking out New York Mets third baseman David Wright to end the top of the third inning. Volquez's father had passed away earlier that day, unbeknownst to him at the time.

Escobar's mad dash

Alcides Escobar swung at the first pitch he saw, and there was nothing unusual about that.

But the result hadn't been seen for decades.

Escobar connected on a Matt Harvey fastball and sent it into the left-field gap, where it landed, and 360 feet later he crossed home plate standing up.

The rarest of baseball plays occurred in the oddest of circumstances - the first pitch the Royals saw in the 111th World Series - and got them off to a fast start in a game that extended into extra innings.

The inside-the-park home run was the first in a World Series game since 1929, and it marked the second time such a feat had opened a Fall Classic game.

Escobar's shot shouldn't have turned into a home run. It appeared that center fielder Yoenis Cespedes and left fielder Michael Conforto miscommunicated as the ball was approaching.

Conforto appeared to stop and give way to Cespedes, who didn't have his glove in a position to grab the ball, which rolled to the wall.

At that point, it looked like a standup double for Escobar. But the ball caromed off Cespedes' foot and rolled along the warning track.

By the time Cespedes had picked it up, Escobar was at third and headed for home.

Escobar has been the team's hottest postseason hitter. The home run extended his playoff hitting streak to 11 games, and he's in pursuit of Lorenzo Cain's consecutive-

game hitting streak of 13, which Cain established this postseason.

This was the Royals' 12th playoff game this year, and Escobar is 11 for 22 (.500) when leading off an inning, including 6 for 11 (.545) when leading off a game. He has now hit for the cycle when leading off a game, notching a single, double and triple leading off games against the Blue Jays. Escobar was chosen MVP for the series.

He got the World Series off to a great start for the Royals.

- *Blair Kerkhoff*

ALLISON LONG

Lorenzo Cain safely stole second past New York Mets shortstop Wilmer Flores in the sixth inning. Mike Moustakas followed with a two-out single that scored Cain and tied the game.

Royals right fielder Paulo Orlando ran for first on a 12th-inning grounder while Mets first baseman Lucas Duda tried to field the ball before it popped out of his glove, giving Orlando a single.

JOE LEDFORD

First baseman Eric Hosmer watched a ball hit by New York Mets shortstop Wilmer Flores fly by him in the eighth inning, which allowed a run to score, giving the Mets the lead 4-3.

Hosmer, Zobrist bust Brett playoff records

Move over, George Brett.

The greatest Royals player of all time and the franchise's only player enshrined in Cooperstown no longer boasts the most career postseason RBIs.

Another of Brett's playoff records was broken Tuesday during the World Series opener at Kauffman Stadium.

First baseman Eric Hosmer's sixth-inning sacrifice fly substantially aided a two-run rally, but it also gave him 24 career RBIs in the playoffs.

That's one more than the 23 RBIs that Brett racked up in 43 postseason games between 1976 and 1985.

In the 14th inning, Hosmer added an RBI with a game-winning sacrifice fly.

Hosmer totaled 12 RBIs in 15 games last season and already has 13 RBIs in 12 games this postseason, with at least three more games guaranteed.

Second baseman Ben Zobrist dashed home on Hosmer's record-breaking sacrifice fly, which came off Mets starter Matt Harvey, a former Midland amateur baseball teammate.

With the Royals trailing 3-1, Zobrist led off the sixth by rolling a double into the right-field corner.

He also led off the eighth inning with a double.

Zobrist now has eight extra-base hits this postseason, one more than Brett socked in nine games during the 1980 playoffs.

Zobrist - whose wife, Julianna, is expecting the couple's third child - needed 12 games to get his record.

Alex Gordon and Mike Moustakas each finished last year's postseason with seven extra-base hits in 15 games.

- Tod Palmer

Pitcher Chris Young finished the game with three scoreless innings and ended up with the victory when Eric Hosmer drove in the winning run in the 14th inning.

Story of the game

BY PETE GRATHOFF

1 It's that Esky magic
Edinson Volquez made swift work of the Mets. Curtis Granderson flied to left, David Wright flied to right and Daniel Murphy, Mr. Home Run, struck out. Alcides Escobar did his thing: He swung at the first pitch. Escobar drove a pitch to the left-field gap, but Mets center fielder Yoenis Cespedes appeared to have a bead on the ball. Then he appeared to try a backhand catch. The ball hit off his foot and skidded away and Escobar rounded the bases on an inside-the-park homer. Eric Hosmer drew a two-out walk, but Kendrys Morales grounded out to third.

1-0
KC-NYM

2 Royals leave two on
The Mets didn't do anything again as Volquez set them down in order. Salvador Perez hit a one-out single and Alex Gordon drew a walk. But Mets starter Matt Harvey got Alex Rios to fly to center and Escobar grounded to third.

1-0
KC-NYM

3 Volquez escapes jam
The Mets had their first threat of the game as Kelly Johnson and Granderson drew consecutive two-out walks. However, Volquez struck out Wright looking and escaped the jam. The Royals went down in order. Hosmer made the third out on a slow grounder to short, despite diving into first base.

1-0
KC-NYM

4 Mets draw even
Murphy opened the inning with a single, and moved to third on a one-out single by Lucas Duda. Travis d'Arnaud also singled and Murphy came in to score as the Mets tied the game. The Royals didn't have a base runner, but Perez was robbed of a hit on a jumping catch by Wright at third base.

1-1
KC-NYM

5 Granderson goes yard
With one out, Granderson hit a home run to right field as the Mets moved ahead. Volquez induced a pair of ground outs to Zobrist to end the top of the inning. The Royals went down in order again as Harvey made it 11 in a row retired.

2-1
NYM-KC

6 All tied up
The Mets padded their lead as Cespedes and Duda opened the frame with singles. Volquez got a big strikeout of d'Arnaud, but Cespedes scored on a sacrifice fly to Gordon in left. The two-run lead vanished quickly. Ben Zobrist turned on a 94-mph fastball and lined a ball into the right-field corner. Lorenzo Cain followed with a single and Zobrist took third. Hosmer's fly to center got Zobrist home. Cain stole second and Moustakas delivered a big two-out single that scored Cain.

3-3
KC-NYM

7 Into the bullpens
Danny Duffy started the inning for the Royals and he struck out pinch hitter Michael Cuddyer and got Granderson to fly to right. Kelvin Herrera entered, and wobbled before he got Cespedes to fly to left. Addison Reed set down the Royals in order.

3-3
KC-NYM

8 One great at-bat for Mets
With two outs, Juan Legares singled and then stole second. Wilmer Flores hit a bouncing ball to Hosmer at first, and he tried to make a backhanded grab of the ball. It got by him and Legares sped home. Zobrist opened the inning with a double off Tyler Clippard. Cain tried unsuccessfully to bunt before striking out. Hosmer also fanned, but Zobrist took third on a wild pitch. Morales then walked and the rally appeared to be on. However, the Mets called on closer Jeurys Familia, who got Moustakas to ground out.

4-3
NYM-KC

9 Gordon to the rescue
Wright had a one-out single off Luke Hochevar, but he was caught stealing. Murphy lifted a lazy fly to center with one out in the ninth. Gordon crushed a home run to straightaway center field to tie it.

4-4
KC-NYM

14 It's an instant classic
Chris Young, the Royals' presumptive Game 4 starter, pitched his third shutout inning. The Royals loaded the bases and Hosmer won it with a sacrifice fly to right that scored Escobar.

5-4
KC-NYM

ROYALS 5, METS 4, 14 INN.

New York	AB	R	H	BI	BB	SO	Avg.
Granderson rf	5	1	1	1	2	0	.200
D.Wright 3b	7	0	2	0	0	2	.286
Dan.Murphy 2b	7	1	2	0	0	2	.286
Cespedes cf-lf	6	1	1	0	0	2	.167
Duda 1b	6	0	2	0	0	3	.333
T.d'Arnaud c	6	0	1	1	0	2	.167
Conforto lf	2	0	0	1	0	0	.000
Lagares cf	3	1	2	0	0	1	.667
W.Flores ss	4	0	0	0	1	0	.000
K.Johnson dh	1	0	0	0	0	0	.000
a-Cuddyer ph-dh	3	0	0	0	0	3	.000
b-Nieuwenhuis ph	1	0	0	0	0	0	.000
Totals	51	4	11	3	3	15	

Kansas City	AB	R	H	BI	BB	SO	Avg.
A.Escobar ss	6	2	1	1	0	0	.167
Zobrist 2b	6	1	3	0	1	0	.500
L.Cain cf	6	1	1	0	1	2	.167
Hosmer 1b	3	0	0	2	2	2	.000
K.Morales dh	3	0	0	0	1	1	.000
1-J.Dyson pr-dh	2	0	0	0	0	0	.000
Moustakas 3b	6	0	2	1	0	0	.333
S.Perez c	6	0	2	0	0	0	.333
A.Gordon lf	5	1	1	1	1	2	.200
Rios rf	3	0	0	0	0	0	.000
Orlando rf	3	0	1	0	0	0	.333
Totals	49	5	11	5	6	7	

Mets	000 111 010 000 00	—	4	11	1
Royals	100 002 001 000 01	—	5	11	1

One out when winning run scored.
1-ran for K.Morales in the 8th.

E: D.Wright (1), Hosmer (1). **LOB:** New York 11, Kansas City 13. **2B:** Zobrist 2 (2). **HR:** Granderson (1), off Volquez; A.Escobar (1), off Harvey; A.Gordon (1), off Familia. **RBIs:** Granderson (1), T.d'Arnaud (1), Conforto (1), A.Escobar (1), Hosmer 2 (2), Moustakas (1), A.Gordon (1). **SB:** Lagares (1), L.Cain (1). **CS:** D.Wright (1). **S:** W.Flores, A.Escobar. **SF:** Conforto, Hosmer 2.

Runners left in scoring position: New York 5 (D.Wright 2, W.Flores 2, Cespedes); Kansas City 5 (A.Escobar, Moustakas, J.Dyson 2, Orlando). **RISP:** New York 1 for 10; Kansas City 2 for 11. **Runners moved up:** L.Cain, A.Gordon.

New York	IP	H	R	ER	BB	SO	NP	ERA
Harvey	6	5	3	3	2	2	80	4.50
A.Reed	1	0	0	0	0	0	12	0.00
Clippard	⅔	1	0	0	1	2	13	0.00
Familia	1⅓	1	1	1	0	0	13	6.75
Niese	2	1	0	0	0	3	21	0.00
B.Colon L, 0-1	2⅓	3	1	0	3	0	50	0.00

Kansas City	IP	H	R	ER	BB	SO	NP	ERA
Volquez	6	6	3	3	1	3	78	4.50
D.Duffy	⅔	0	0	0	0	1	14	0.00
K.Herrera	1⅓	3	1	0	0	2	35	0.00
Hochevar	1	1	0	0	0	0	8	0.00
W.Davis	1	0	0	0	0	3	18	0.00
Madson	1	1	0	0	1	2	22	0.00
C.Young W, 1-0	3	0	0	0	1	4	53	0.00

Hold: Clippard (1). **Blown save:** Familia (1). **Inherited runners-scored:** Familia 2-0. **IBB:** off B.Colon (Zobrist, Hosmer, L.Cain). **HBP:** by Volquez (K.Johnson). **WP:** Clippard.

Umpires: Home, Bill Welke; First, Mark Carlson; Second, Mike Winters; Third, Jim Wolf; Left, Alfonso Marquez; Right, Gary Cederstrom. **Time:** 5:09. **Att:** 40,320.

Royals players celebrated with first baseman Eric Hosmer after he hit a sacrifice fly in the 14th inning to drive in Alcides Escobar for the winning run.

Royals relief pitcher Kelvin Herrera entered in the seventh inning and gave up just one unearned run in the eighth when Eric Hosmer booted a ground ball off the bat of Wilmer Flores.

Relief pitcher Danny Duffy clapped after he walked off the field after being relieved in the seventh inning.

Royals starting pitcher
Johnny Cueto celebrated
with shortstop Alcides
Escobar on his way to a
one-run, two-hit mastery
of the Mets in Game 2.

JOHN SLEEZER

WORLD SERIES
GAME 2

	123	456	789	R	H	E
New York	000	100	000 —	1	2	1
Kansas City	000	040	03x —	7	10	0

W W 3 4 5 6 7

THE KANSAS CITY STAR

10/29/15

Just two much fun

....

Cueto limits Mets to a couple of hits in 7-1 complete-game victory

....

KC batters jump on New York starter Jacob deGrom with four-run fifth inning

....

———————

BY ANDY McCULLOUGH

Kauffman Stadium may never feel better than this, not in 2015, not in a lifetime. For the inhabitants of this ballpark, stocked with a generation of Royals fans choked by 29 years without October and taunted by a silver medal in 2014, the pinnacle may have come in a 7-1 victory Wednesday over the Mets in Game 2 of the World Series, when the lineup bloodied an opposing ace and incited a slew of standing ovations.

Savor this if you stood among the rain-soaked mass of 40,410 inside the stadium. Savor it if you joined the millions watching on television or huddling near a radio. Savor it if you spent years waiting for a Royals renaissance, because baseball might not be played again in Kansas City this season.

Baseball may disappear for the sweetest of reasons, because the Royals flew to New York on Wednesday night with a chance to spill champagne inside Citi Field for their first championship since 1985. A four-run fifth inning carried Kansas City to a 2-0 lead in this series. The rally acted like a season-long highlight reel in miniature, a collection of good fortune, well-placed hits and tenacious at-bats.

The Royals peppered Jacob deGrom, New York's long-haired staff leader, with jabs and hooks. In three starts this October, deGrom had yielded only four runs. The Royals managed that many in the fifth inning alone.

Trailing by a run when the inning began, Alcides Escobar

JOHN SLEEZER

The Royals' Mike Moustakas was pumped up after he hit an RBI single in the fifth inning of Game 2.

failed to lay down a bunt, so he responded by tying the game with a two-strike single up the middle. Eric Hosmer pushed his club in front with a two-run hit. Mike Moustakas completed the flurry with an RBI single of his own.

In a fit of brilliance, Johnny Cueto protected the lead with the first two-hit complete game in the World Series since Greg Maddux twirled one for Atlanta in 1995. Cueto retired 15 batters in a row after giving up a run in the fourth. The ballpark showered him with adoration, a far cry from the derision he faced last week in Canada.

The team hoped by affording Cueto a chance to pitch at home, in a ballpark he credits as a source of vitality, spacious confines and a friendly crowd could assuage whatever ails him, be it contractual anxiety, worries about the health of his right elbow or a general lack of comfort.

In deGrom, Cueto found a worthy rival. The duo traded zeros at the start. Cueto faced the minimum through three innings. DeGrom saw 10 batters, but did not allow a hit.

Cueto personified efficiency during those three innings. He lost acquaintance with the strike zone in the fourth. Umpire Mark Carlson ceased giving Cueto the corners. A run resulted from it.

Curtis Granderson led off with a walk. Cueto threw three balls in a row to David Wright before Wright hit a foul pop-up. Daniel Murphy accepted a second walk to set the table for Yoenis Cespedes.

Cespedes sent a grounder hopping toward third base. Moustakas stepped on the bag for one out. He could have ended the inning, but his throw yanked first baseman Hosmer off his bag, his toe just inches away from a third out.

The replay looked inconclusive. Yost peered into his dugout, where bench coach Don Wakamatsu waited on the phone for a decision from the team's replay coordinator, Bill Duplissea. The Royals decided not to challenge.

At times in Game 1, Kansas City unveiled an exaggerated defensive shift for Lucas Duda, New York's left-handed, pull-hitting first baseman. Moustakas ventured over to the far side of second base. Duda still pulled a pair of hits through the defense. In the view of some team officials, he capitalized on the awkwardness of the alignment.

The Royals debated the merits of the shift heading into Game 2. Moustakas remained on the left side of third in Duda's at-bat in the second, but Duda still threaded a single through the area vacated by shortstop Escobar. In Duda's next at-bat, he found another way to vex the Royals. He flared a single over Moustakas' head to score Murphy.

Kansas City answered in the fifth. The first man up was Alex Gordon. The night before, he conquered closer Jeurys Familia with a game-tying homer in the bottom of the ninth. Now he took a walk, and advanced to second on a single by Alex Rios.

Up came Escobar. In these situations, for years, he has dropped down bunts. He believes it is his responsibility to move the runners into scoring position, not to bring them home. But he could not square up deGrom, who fired a pair of fastballs to start.

Down two strikes, Escobar forced himself to hit. It was a wise choice. He rifled a hanging slider into center field and drove in Gordon.

The pitch location from deGrom was a harbinger. He could not drive the baseball down toward the knees. The Royals feasted on him. As Mets lefty Jon Niese heated up in the bullpen, Collins stuck with deGrom against Hosmer. DeGrom threw another flat slider. Hosmer punched it into center for two runs.

Moustakas offered an exclamation point. In typical fashion, he did not provide thunder. Instead he pounced on a toothless curveball and threaded it through the infield to score Hosmer.

The Royals tacked on a trio of runs in the eighth, thanks to lackluster defending by the Mets. The fans pumped their fists and shredded their lungs. Inside this park, parties have raged all season long. The franchise shattered its record for attendance. The players overcame the stigma of being a one-year wonder.

So savor this night, just as you savored all the nights before it, through the long years and the lean years, through the heartbreak of last October. Savor the 2015 Royals. Because when the team returns to Kansas City next week, you may not see any baseball. You may have to settle for a parade.

JOE LEDFORD

KC's RBI machine

Hosmer has made coming through with men on base a habit, driving in a team-record 15 runs so far in the postseason

When Eric Hosmer has stepped to the plate with the bases empty during the postseason, he's been a bust.

He struck out in his first plate appearance Wednesday, leading off the second inning, dropping his batting average in those situations to .043, with 1 hit in 23 at-bats.

But put runners on, especially in scoring position, and Hosmer becomes a beast.

His two-run single was the decisive blow in the sixth inning of the Royals' 7-1 victory over the Mets in Game 2 of the World Series.

The single up the middle with two outs against Mets starter Jacob deGrom scored Alex Rios and Alcides Escobar and broke a 1-1 tie, sending the Royals on their way to a 2-0 lead in the World Series that shifts to New York for Game 3 on Friday.

The two RBIs gave Hosmer four in two World Series games and 15 for the playoffs, padding team record totals. The 15 RBIs are the most by a Royals player in a single postseason, and he continues to add to his career record, which now stands at 27.

Hosmer's playoff batting average with runners on in the playoffs stands at .379 (11 for 29).

"Anytime you have opportunities with guys on base you have to make the most of it," Hosmer said. "You see everybody bear down, put together good at-bats and fight off tough pitchers' pitches."

Nobody is doing it better than Hosmer.

- Blair Kerkhoff

JOHN SLEEZER

Alcides Escobar slid into home past Mets catcher Travis d'Arnaud as Eric Hosmer knocked in two runs in the fifth inning of the Royals' 7-1 win in Game 2 of the World Series.

Alex Gordon hit a double and drove in a run in the eighth inning.

SHANE KEYSER

Royals shortstop Alcides Escobar fielded and threw to first on a grounder by New York Mets center fielder Juan Lagares for the final out of the eighth inning during Game 2 of the World Series.

Catcher Salvador Perez hugged pitcher Johnny Cueto after he completed his two-hitter.

Salvador Perez doused Johnny Cueto with ice water after Cueto pitched a complete game for a 7-1 win over the New York Mets.

Story of the game

BY PETE GRATHOFF

1 Cueto looks good

Johnny Cueto had a nice start. Curtis Granderson and David Wright grounded out, and Daniel Murphy struck out looking. The Royals went down in order - all on fly balls to Granderson in right.

0-0
KC-NYM

2 Nice double play

Lucas Duda singled with one out as Mike Moustakas ranged far to his left while already shifted in that direction. But Travis d'Arnaud hit into a 5-4-3 double play. The Royals again failed to reach base against Mets starter Jacob deGrom.

0-0
KC-NYM

3 Royals get first base runner

After Cueto retired all three Mets, Alex Gordon drew a one-out walk. However, Alex Rios struck out and Alcides Escobar grounded into a fielder's choice that forced Rios at second.

0-0
KC-NYM

4 Mets take the lead

Granderson opened the frame with a walk. After Wright popped out to Eric Hosmer at first base, Murphy also walked. Yoenis Cespedes grounded to Moustakas at third base. He stepped on the bag, but his throw to first pulled Hosmer off the base. That allowed Granderson to score. The Royals threatened as Ben Zobrist reached on an error and moved to second on a single by Hosmer. Both runners moved up a base on Kendrys Morales' grounder to first. Moustakas walked and loaded the bases. But Salvador Perez grounded to short.

1-0
NYM-KC

5 Keep the line moving

Cueto buzzed through the Mets with little trouble, and then the Royals went to work. Gordon led off with a walk and Rios singled. Escobar failed in a bunt attempt and instead had an RBI single to center that scored Gordon. Zobrist's grounder to first moved runners to second and third. Lorenzo Cain hit a liner to center, and the runners had to stay put. Hosmer came through with a line-drive single to center that scored Rios and Escobar and put the Royals ahead. But they weren't done. Morales and Moustakas also singled, with the latter hit scoring Hosmer.

4-1
KC-NYM

6 Nothing doing

Mets postseason star Murphy struck out and ended another 1-2-3 inning by Cueto, which was met with approval from the 40,410 at Kauffman Stadium. The Mets turned to Hansel Robles, and although a couple of balls were hit hard, the Royals didn't have a base runner.

4-1
KC-NYM

7 A perfect 10

Cueto continued to baffle the Mets, striking out Cespedes, and getting Duda and d'Arnaud to hit fly balls. That made it 10 straight Mets that Cueto had set down. Jon Niese relieved for the Mets, and he gave up a one-out walk to Cain. However, Hosmer flied out and Morales struck out.

4-1
KC-NYM

8 Royals do it with defense, offense

Cueto returned for the eighth and as far as the Mets were concerned, it was more of the same. But he did get some help from the defense. Wilmer Flores hit a liner that Moustakas snagged. Then Juan Lagares hit a ball off Cueto that Escobar made a nice play on, getting the ball and throwing to first. Moustakas opened the inning with a single past Duda at first and Perez yanked a double down the third-base line. With the infield drawn in a bit, Gordon hit a ball that Flores couldn't quite field and it turned into an RBI double. Paulo Orlando's sacrifice fly scored Perez, and Escobar tripled to center as Gordon trotted home.

7-1
KC-NYM

9 Cueto's gem complete

The crowd serenaded Cueto before he came out of the dugout. He finally appeared and skipped over the foul line on his way to the mound. He then induced grounders from Granderson and Wright. Murphy walked, but Cespedes flied to right. It was a wonderful performance from Cueto.

7-1
KC-NYM

ROYALS 7, METS 1

New York	AB	R	H	BI	BB	SO	Avg.
Granderson rf	3	0	0	0	1	0	.125
D.Wright 3b	4	0	0	0	0	0	.182
Dan.Murphy 2b	2	1	0	0	2	2	.222
Cespedes lf	4	0	0	0	0	1	.100
Duda 1b	3	0	2	1	0	0	.444
T.d'Arnaud c	3	0	0	0	0	0	.111
Conforto dh	3	0	0	0	0	1	.000
W.Flores ss	3	0	0	0	0	0	.000
Lagares cf	3	0	0	0	0	0	.333
Totales	28	1	2	1	3	4	

Kansas City	AB	R	H	BI	BB	SO	Avg.
A.Escobar ss	5	1	2	2	0	0	.273
Zobrist 2b	5	0	0	0	0	0	.273
L.Cain cf	4	0	0	0	1	0	.100
Hosmer 1b	4	1	2	2	0	1	.286
K.Morales dh	4	0	1	0	0	1	.143
Moustakas 3b	3	1	2	1	1	0	.444
S.Perez c	4	1	1	0	0	0	.300
A.Gordon lf	2	2	1	1	2	0	.286
Rios rf	3	1	1	0	0	1	.167
Orlando rf	0	0	0	1	0	0	.333
Totals	34	7	10	7	4	3	

New York	000	100	000	—	1	2	1
Kansas City	000	040	03x	—	7	10	0

E: Duda (1). **LOB:** New York 3, Kansas City 8. **2B:** S.Perez (1), A.Gordon (1). **3B:** A.Escobar (1). **RBIs:** Duda (1), A.Escobar 2 (3), Hosmer 2 (4), Moustakas (2), A.Gordon (2), Orlando (1). **SF:** Orlando.

Runners left in scoring position: New York 2 (T.d'Arnaud, Cespedes); Kansas City 4 (S.Perez 3, L.Cain). **RISP:** New York 1 for 4; Kansas City 5 for 12. **Runners moved up:** Zobrist, K.Morales. **GIDP:** T.d'Arnaud. **DP:** Kansas City 1 (Moustakas, Zobrist, Hosmer).

New York	IP	H	R	ER	BB	SO	NP	ERA
deGrom L, 0-1	5	6	4	4	3	2	94	7.20
Robles	1	0	0	0	0	0	11	0.00
Niese	1	3	3	3	1	1	27	9.00
A.Reed	⅓	1	0	0	0	0	6	0.00
Gilmartin	⅔	0	0	0	0	0	4	0.00

Kansas City	IP	H	R	ER	BB	SO	NP	ERA
Cueto W, 1-0	9	2	1	1	3	4	122	1.00

Niese pitched to 3 batters in the 8th.

Inherited runners-scored: A.Reed 2-2, Gilmartin 1-0.

Umpires: Home, Mark Carlson; First, Mike Winters; Second, Jim Wolf; Third, Alfonso Marquez; Left, Gary Cederstrom; Right, Bill Welke. **Time:** 2:54. **Att:** 40,410.

Royals pitcher Yordano Ventura rubbed a baseball as Mets outfielder Curtis Granderson crossed home plate after hitting a two-run home run in the third inning of Game 3.

DAVID EULITT

WORLD SERIES GAME 3

	123	456	789	R	H	E
Kansas City	120	000	000 —	3	7	0
New York	202	104	00x —	9	12	0

W W L 4 5 6 7

THE KANSAS CITY STAR

10/31/15

Flushing sound

....

Ventura's radar-gun numbers down as pitches fly out in 9-3 loss to Mets

....

Hard-throwing Syndergaard doesn't dominate but gets the win

....

————————

BY ANDY McCULLOUGH

NEW YORK

The first thing Ned Yost locates inside a ballpark is the scoreboard's radar gun. The numbers help him discern from the dugout the pitch selection and viability of his staff.

Here at Citi Field, where the Royals took part in Game 3 of the World Series, the readings flash on a screen high above the right-field fence, framed in the foreground as jets cruise over Flushing Bay into LaGuardia Airport.

In the second and third innings of a 9-3 loss to the Mets, which reduced Kansas City to a 2-1 advantage in the Fall Classic, a curiously low batch of numbers rolled across the screen, numbers that rarely appear when Yordano Ventura is on the mound: 92, 93, 94. The radar gun foretold Ventura's doom, as he surrendered a pair of two-run homers and failed to complete the fourth inning.

The matchup on Friday was marketed as a duel between young flamethrowers. Only one showed up. Noah Syndergaard, a 23-year-old rookie from Texas, survived two flurries from the Royals and struck out six across six innings.

Ventura collected 10 outs and gave up five runs. As the game crumbled around him in the fourth, Ventura neglected to cover first base, the sort of error that looks more egregious on the game's largest stage. On this platform last season, in Game 2 and Game 6 of the World Series against San Francisco, Ventura allowed only two runs in 12⅓ innings.

DAVID EULITT

Royals pitcher Franklin Morales (left) talked with shortstop Alcides Escobar after a fielding blunder.

A year later, he looked vulnerable from the start and never stifled the charge of the Mets.

After Ventura left the game, Franklin Morales offered a miniaturized meltdown. He gave up a single, hit a batter, allowed an RBI single to pinch hitter Juan Uribe and committed a baffling mistake in which he failed to throw to any base after fielding a comebacker. Reliever Kelvin Herrera could not put out the fire. He gave up a two-run single to David Wright and a sacrifice fly to Yoenis Cespedes, completing a four-run Mets rally.

Syndergaard allowed five hits or fewer in both of his first two starts this postseason. He gave up only four runs total. In the first two innings Friday, the Royals piled up six hits and scored three times. He looked wobbly until suddenly he wasn't. Before Mike Moustakas recorded an infield single in the sixth, Syndergaard had retired 12 in a row.

Syndergaard hinted Thursday that he had a plan to face Alcides Escobar, Kansas City's free-swinging leadoff man. Escobar had offered at the first pitch he saw in his last eight games. Syndergaard joked he had "a few tricks up my sleeve" to combat Escobar.

He was not kidding. To open the evening, Syndergaard whipped a 98-mph fastball toward Escobar's chin. Escobar dived into the dirt. The baseball rattled to the backstop. The crowd howled.

The gesture from Syndergaard - try and hit this - did not go unnoticed. The television cameras captured Moustakas hurling expletives at Syndergaard from the bench. After Escobar struck out, Ben Zobrist walloped a double off the center-field wall. He would score thanks to heady base running and imprecise fielding by the Mets.

With Zobrist bouncing at second, Lorenzo Cain tapped a grounder back toward the mound. The baseball rolled underneath Syndergaard's bare hand. When Wright charged from third, Zobrist advanced 90 feet. Across the diamond, Cain was safe, too.

Eric Hosmer lugged his .231 postseason average with him to the plate. In fitting fashion, he did not get a hit. But he would drive in a run. Hosmer rolled a grounder to first baseman Lucas Duda, who fed shortstop Wilmer Flores for an out at second. Syndergaard failed to reach first base to complete the double play. He still caught the ball and swiped a tag, which connected with Duda and sent him tumbling to the ground.

As a response, the Mets leaned upon their captain, Wright. He is the last connection to his franchise's division-winning club in 2006 and also suffered through six consecutive losing seasons. In his first-ever World Series at-bat at Citi Field, as Curtis Granderson stood at first base, Wright battered a 96-mph fastball that carried over the left-field wall.

The Royals did not roll over. They opened the second with singles from Salvador Perez, Alex Gordon and Alex Rios. The last scored Perez, but Gordon was thrown out trying to go from first to third. Rios reached second on the throw.

That meant Ventura would bat in the playoffs for the first time. He dropped down a clean bunt on an 0-1 fastball, sending Rios to third base. The extra 90 feet was a boon for the Royals. Rios scored when catcher Travis d'Arnaud could not smother a curveball in the dirt.

Ventura retired the side in order in the bottom of the second. The only reason for concern was the radar gun. His fastball did not top 94 mph.

An inning later, Ventura pumped two fastballs to Syndergaard for strikes. His next choice backfired. Ventura sped up Syndergaard's bat with a curveball. Syndergaard smacked a single into center.

Ventura hit 94 mph on a 2-1 fastball, but the location betrayed him. Granderson hammered the thigh-high heater down the right-field line. The ball only traveled an estimated 347 feet, but far enough to scrape over the wall and give the Mets the lead.

The Mets overpowered Ventura in the fourth. Duda led off with a single, and d'Arnaud hammered a 93-mph fastball for a double. Duda held at third, and pitching coach Dave Eiland visited the mound to settle Ventura down. The message did not take.

After talking to Eiland, Ventura induced a grounder off the bat off rookie outfielder Michael Conforto. Hosmer strayed to his right to field it. He left the bag vacant. Ventura idled near the third-base line, making no movement to cover the base. A run would have scored regardless, but now Conforto received credit for a single.

Ventura's night ended one batter later. Danny Duffy stranded two batters, and Luke Hochevar spun a scoreless fifth inning. But for the sixth, Yost chose Morales over another inning from Hochevar, a clean start for Herrera or even an extended stint from Kris Medlen. The Mets pounced on Morales, reduced him to rubble and earned a chance to even this series tonight.

DAVID EULITT

A throw pulled Royals first baseman Eric Hosmer off the bag, and the Mets' Curtis Granderson reached on a single.

The first pitch of Game 3 on Friday night was never intended to be hit by Royals shortstop Alcides Escobar, who had to duck when the ball buzzed his head.

DAVID EULITT

Mets right fielder Curtis Granderson and starting pitcher Noah Syndergaard (right) celebrated in front of Royals catcher Salvador Perez after Granderson homered in the third inning of Game 3 of the World Series in New York.

JOHN SLEEZER

Royals doomed by silly fielding gaffes

Franklin Morales' mistake in sixth inning opens the door to a big Mets inning

JOE LEDFORD

NEW YORK

In the span of 3 seconds - a spinning, indecisive, manic 3 seconds - reliever Franklin Morales let Game 3 of this World Series slip through his unsure fingers.

Here was the scene: In the bottom of the sixth inning, with the Royals still within striking distance, Morales worked with runners at the corners, coaxing a comebacker from Mets outfielder Curtis Granderson. Morales, a left-hander, immediately spun to second, where a strong throw could have started an inning-ending double play.

But then Morales inexplicably turned back toward home plate, looking Wilmer Flores back to third. By the time Morales turned back toward second, peeking at third in the process, Juan Uribe was bearing down toward second. Morales could only uncork an off-balance throw that spiked into the dirt wide of second and found a surprised Ben Zobrist, who was backing up the play.

Just like that, the Mets had the bases loaded, Morales' night was done, and the Mets would soon bust open the game on a two-run single from third baseman David Wright. Morales, who recorded just one out, was charged with four runs and two hits, exacerbating the damage after a shaky start from Yordano Ventura, who allowed five earned runs in 3⅓ innings and had his own defensive wobble in the fourth.

After allowing a single and a double opening the inning, Ventura got Michael Conforto to hit a chopper to the hole at second. First baseman Eric Hosmer ranged to his right, fielding the ball, but Ventura did not cover first base, and Conforto was safe with an RBI infield single.

- Rustin Dodd

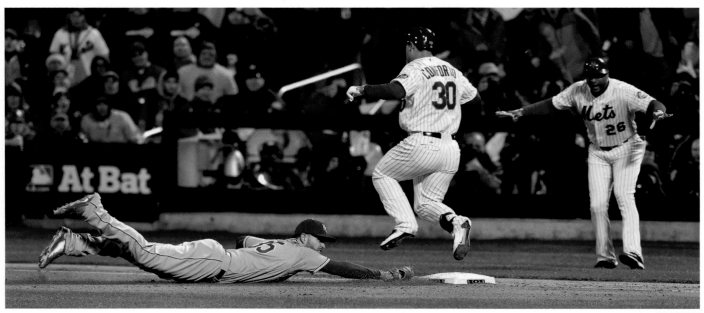

DAVID EULITT

A misplay in the fourth inning led to Royals first baseman Eric Hosmer scrambling to tag the base, but he was late getting there and Mets left fielder Michael Conforto had an infield single.

Story of the game

BY PETE GRATHOFF

1 Crazy start
Noah Syndergaard made sure Alcides Escobar didn't swing at the first pitch - Syndergaard threw a pitch near Escobar's head, and Escobar later struck out. But Ben Zobrist doubled and took third on Lorenzo Cain's dribbler past the mound. Eric Hosmer grounded to first baseman Lucas Duda, whose throw forced Cain, but a mixup on the throw back to first allowed Hosmer to reach and Zobrist to score. The Mets responded quickly: Curtis Granderson singled off Yordano Ventura, and David Wright homered to left-center field.

2-1
NYM-KC

2 Back come the Royals
Salvador Perez hit a looper behind third base and took second on Alex Gordon's single. Alex Rios doubled to left, and that scored Perez. However, Gordon was thrown out at third on a nice play by left fielder Michael Conforto. Ventura sacrificed Rios to third, and Rios scored on a passed ball. The Mets didn't have a base runner in their half.

3-2
KC-NYM

3 Another Mets homer
The Royals were put down in order by Syndergaard, and then he led off with a single for New York. Granderson yanked a ball into the right-field seats by the foul pole and gave the Mets the lead.

4-3
NYM-KC

4 Duffy puts out fire
After the Royals went down in order again, Duda had a leadoff single for the Mets. Catcher Travis d'Arnaud doubled into the left-field corner. Conforto singled home Duda to increase the Mets' lead. Ventura got Wilmer Flores to pop to Hosmer in foul territory, but Ned Yost brought on Danny Duffy. He struck out Syndergaard and got Granderson on a fly ball to Cain.

5-3
NYM-KC

5 Here's Hochevar
Syndergaard clearly had shaken off his earlier troubles, and he again retired the Royals without allowing a runner. Luke Hochevar relieved for the Royals. He gave up a two-out single but struck out Duda to end the inning.

5-3
NYM-KC

6 Missed chance and no relief
With two outs, the Royals finally got on base against Syndergaard. Mike Moustakas singled, and Perez walked. After Gordon walked and loaded the bases, Syndergaard got Rios to ground out to short-stop. Franklin Morales entered and things turned ugly. With one out, pinch hitter Juan Lagares singled, and then Wilmer Flores was hit by a pitch. Juan Uribe, another pinch hitter, singled and Lagares scored. Granderson hit a ball back to Morales. Morales looked at second. He looked at home plate. He looked at third base. Then he turned back to second and threw wildly. Everybody was safe, and the bases were loaded. Kelvin Herrera replaced Morales, but Daniel Murphy had a two-run single and Yoenis Cespedes hit a sacrifice fly.

9-3
NYM-KC

7 Nothing happening here
Addison Reed took the mound for the Mets and had a 1-2-3 inning. Ryan Madson relieved for the Royals and allowed a leadoff single to d'Arnaud. However, Lagares flied out, Flores grounded to Moustakas, who threw to second and forced d'Arnaud. Kirk Nieuwenhuis pinch hit and struck out.

9-3
NYM-KC

8 Medlen's debut
Now it was Tyler Clippard's turn to pitch for the Mets, and he got Cain to pop out, Hosmer to fly to center and Moustakas to pop to ... Clippard. Kris Medlen made his World Series debut and got the Mets in order with two strikeouts.

9-3
NYM-KC

9 Can't win them all
In what was obviously not a save situation, the Mets called on closer Jeurys Familia. He was the guy who served up Gordon's game-tying homer in Game 1. This time he struck out Gordon as part of another 1-2-3 inning for the Mets.

9-3
NYM-KC

METS 9, ROYALS 3

Kansas City	AB	R	H	BI	BB	SO	Avg.
A.Escobar ss	4	0	1	0	0	2	.267
Zobrist 2b	4	1	1	0	0	0	.267
L.Cain cf	4	0	1	0	0	1	.143
Hosmer 1b	4	0	0	1	0	1	.182
Moustakas 3b	4	0	1	0	0	0	.385
S.Perez c	3	1	1	0	1	0	.308
A.Gordon lf	3	0	1	0	1	2	.300
Rios rf	3	1	1	1	0	0	.222
K.Herrera p	0	0	0	0	0	0	---
Madson p	0	0	0	0	0	0	---
Medlen p	0	0	0	0	0	0	---
e-K.Morales ph	1	0	0	0	0	0	.125
Ventura p	0	0	0	0	0	0	---
D.Duffy p	0	0	0	0	0	0	---
a-Mondesi ph	1	0	0	0	0	1	.000
Hochevar p	0	0	0	0	0	0	---
F.Morales p	0	0	0	0	0	0	---
Orlando rf	1	0	0	0	0	0	.250
Totals	32	3	7	2	2	7	

New York	AB	R	H	BI	BB	SO	Avg.
Granderson rf	5	3	2	2	0	0	.231
D.Wright 3b	5	1	2	4	0	2	.250
Dan.Murphy 2b	4	0	0	0	1	1	.154
Cespedes cf-lf	3	0	1	1	0	1	.154
Duda 1b	4	1	1	0	0	2	.385
T.d'Arnaud c	4	0	2	0	0	0	.231
Conforto lf	2	0	1	1	0	0	.143
b-Lagares ph-cf	2	1	1	0	0	0	.375
W.Flores ss	3	1	0	0	0	0	.000
Syndergaard p	2	1	1	0	0	1	.500
c-Uribe ph	1	1	1	1	0	0	1.000
A.Reed p	0	0	0	0	0	0	---
d-Nieuwenhuis ph	1	0	0	0	1	0	.000
Clippard p	0	0	0	0	0	0	---
Familia p	0	0	0	0	0	0	---
Totals	36	9	12	9	1	8	

Kansas City	120	000	000	—	3	7 0
New York	202	104	00x	—	9	12 0

a-struck out for D.Duffy in the 5th. b-singled for Conforto in the 6th. c-singled for Syndergaard in the 6th. d-struck out for A.Reed in the 7th. e-grounded out for Medlen in the 9th.

LOB: Kansas City 5, New York 6. **2B:** Zobrist (3), T.d'Arnaud (1). **HR:** D.Wright (1), off Ventura; Granderson (2), off Ventura. **RBIs:** Hosmer (5), Rios (1), Granderson 2 (3), D.Wright 4 (4), Cespedes (1), Conforto (2), Uribe (1). **SB:** A.Escobar (1). **S:** Ventura. **SF:** Cespedes.

Runners left in scoring position: Kansas City 3 (Zobrist, Rios 2); New York 2 (Granderson, Duda). **RISP:** Kansas City 2 for 5; New York 3 for 8.

Kansas City	IP	H	R	ER	BB	SO	NP	ERA
Ventura L, 0-1	3⅓	7	5	5	0	1	53	13.50
D.Duffy	⅔	0	0	0	1	1	10	0.00
Hochevar	1	1	0	0	0	2	15	0.00
F.Morales	⅓	2	4	4	0	0	22	108.00
K.Herrera	⅔	1	0	0	1	1	16	0.00
Madson	1	1	0	0	0	1	15	0.00
Medlen	1	0	0	0	0	2	15	0.00

New York	IP	H	R	ER	BB	SO	NP	ERA
Syndergaard W, 1-0	6	7	3	3	2	6	104	4.50
A.Reed	1	0	0	0	0	0	12	0.00
Clippard	1	0	0	0	0	0	13	0.00
Familia	1	0	0	0	0	1	13	1.86

Inherited runners-scored: D.Duffy 2-0, K.Herrera 3-3. **HBP:** by F.Morales (W.Flores). **PB:** T.d'Arnaud.

Umpires: Home, Mike Winters; First, Jim Wolf; Second, Alfonso Marquez; Third, Gary Cederstrom; Left, Mike Everitt; Right, Mark Carlson. **Time:** 3:22. **Att:** 44,781.

Royals first baseman Eric Hosmer celebrated with shortstop Alcides Escobar after scoring in the eighth inning of Game 4 of the World Series on Saturday in New York.

JOHN SLEEZER

WORLD SERIES GAME 4

	123	456	789	R	H	E
Kansas City	000	011	030 —	5	9	0
New York	002	010	000 —	3	6	2

W W L W 5 6 7

THE KANSAS CITY STAR

11/1/15

Hallo-wheee!

....

Royals score three runs in the inning and beat the Mets 5-3 in Game 4 of the World Series

....

They collect two hits, two walks and take advantage of an error

....

_____

BY ANDY McCULLOUGH

NEW YORK

The beginning always looks so harmless. That's the thing. These Royals, winners again in Game 4 of the World Series, a 5-3 triumph over the Mets, never burst into a room. Their opponents cannot recognize the danger until it is too late.

So when Ben Zobrist chucked his bat toward the Kansas City dugout on Saturday evening, there was little reason for panic at Citi Field. Zobrist represented the tying run after walking with one out in the eighth inning, but the Mets had stifled the Royals all evening. Looming in the bullpen was their fearsome closer, Jeurys Familia. The Mets were five outs away from tying this series.

The door peeked open a crack when Mets reliever Tyler Clippard walked Lorenzo Cain. Into the breach came Familia. Eric Hosmer chopped a grounder toward second base. And the arc of this series bent toward Kansas City.

The baseball slipped beneath the glove of Mets second baseman Daniel Murphy. He played the hero during the first two rounds of these playoffs. Now he served as the goat. The error allowed Zobrist to score and tie the game. Mike Moustakas and Salvador Perez gave the Royals the lead with a pair of RBI singles.

There was no crushing blow, no baseball destined to clear the fences. Two walks. Two hits. A pivotal error. Champions can be crowned on the back of such events.

"They can do a lot of things and they're athletic," Mets

DAVID EULITT

Daniel Murphy had been a New York hero in the earlier rounds of the postseason, but his bat's gone cold and this misplayed dribbler allowed KC to score the tying run Saturday.

manager Terry Collins said. "You have to make your pitches and get outs when you have the opportunity."

The sequence turned this ballpark, rollicking and rolling with orange towels flapping through the air, into a tomb. The undertaker arrived in the form of Wade Davis. He authored a six-out save and pushed the Mets to the brink.

"We feel like if we can keep the game close, we're going to find a way to win it," Royals manager Ned Yost said. "Our bullpen is so dynamic, they give us a chance to win those types of games. And it's a team that just looks for a little crack. If we find a little crack, they're going to make something happen."

Starter Chris Young and Danny Duffy combined to surrender a pair of home runs to rookie outfielder Michael Conforto. A mental lapse by right fielder Alex Rios contributed to a Mets run.

Neither starting pitcher provided much distance. Yost removed Young for a pinch hitter in the top of the fifth. Young had given up two runs. An RBI single by Cain removed Mets rookie Steven Matz from the game in the sixth. Matz yielded two runs across five innings.

The lone, lingering artifact on Saturday from Game 3 was the first pitch of the evening, the chin music from Noah Syndergaard toward Alcides Escobar. A day later, Syndergaard refused to back down from his postgame stance, when he said the pitch was premeditated.

But Young did not hunt the heads of his former New York teammates. Instead he yielded two runs in the third due to a home run and a slate of defensive incompetence.

Conforto supplied the homer on a waist-high, 87-mph fastball. He hammered a towering drive into the second deck of right field on the inning's first pitch. It was the first hit of the game for the Mets and the third hit of the postseason for Conforto.

Wilmer Flores splashed a single into center. As Matz squared to bunt, Young spiked a fastball in the dirt. The ball bounced away and Flores took second. Matz bunted him to third, setting the stage for another mental gaffe by a Royal.

The sequence looked preposterous. Curtis Granderson lifted a fly ball into right. Rios settled underneath it. He relaxed his body as the ball reached his glove. When he caught it, he paused for a moment and took two jogging steps toward the dugout. His body conveyed the universal language of a completed inning.

Except there were only two outs. Rios realized in time to heave the baseball home. There was no play. The Royals challenged the call, suggesting Flores failed to tag up properly and left early. The replay officials upheld the call.

To that point, the Royals could not touch Matz, a 24-year-old lefty pitching in only his ninth major-league game. Matz faced only one batter more than the minimum through four. He struck out five during that time. But his arm slot dropped and his energy lagged as the evening continued.

Kansas City halved the deficit in the fifth. They benefited from a mistake in center by Yoenis Cespedes. He took an inexact route for a liner from Perez, which he kicked into a double. Alex Gordon roped a single into right to score the run.

With two outs and Gordon at first, Yost decided to gamble. Near the on-deck circle, Young dropped his bat and pulled on a sweatshirt. His night was over. Kendrys Morales would pinch hit for him.

In a vacuum, the move worked. Morales roped a single up the middle. There were two men on for Escobar, who lined out to right. But now Young was out of the game, and the Royals had used their most dangerous pinch hitter.

With Young done, Duffy entered the fray. He flung two fastballs for strikes to Conforto. Then he abandoned the heater in favor of his breaking ball. On the third consecutive curveball, Conforto drilled the bender over the right-center fence. Rios scaled the wall but could not retrieve the ball.

The Royals continued to have success against Matz in the sixth. Zobrist tied a record with his eighth double this postseason. Cain rolled a single up the middle to score him.

In came Jon Niese, a southpaw who spent much of the year as a starter. He retired Hosmer and Moustakas. Hosmer stung a ball to center, but it veered right at Cespedes.

Next came burly right-hander Bartolo Colon to face Perez. During a 10-pitch duel, Colon threw only one definitive strike. Perez swung through a slider for the third out.

Catcher Salvador Perez celebrated after his single drove in the final run in the Royals' eighth-inning rally Saturday.

JOHN SLEEZER

DAVID EULITT

Royals fans celebrated after second baseman Ben Zobrist scored on a ball hit by Eric Hosmer in the eighth inning of Game 4 at Citi Field in New York.

Double trouble for Mets

NEW YORK

The top two in the Royals' batting order continue to pile up the playoff numbers, and win postseason games.

Leadoff hitter Alcides Escobar and No. 2 hitter Ben Zobrist did what they do best in the batter's box in the Royals' 5-3 victory over the Mets in Game 4 of the World Series on Saturday.

Escobar led off the game with a sharp single up the middle. It wasn't on the first pitch, as it often has been during the playoffs. That was a swing and a miss.

But with two strikes, Escobar lashed a single to center and extended his postseason hitting streak to 14.

That's a Royals record. Escobar had been tied with Lorenzo Cain, whose 13-game streak extended over two seasons and ended in Game 5 of the American League Championship Series against the Blue Jays.

Escobar went hitless in the Royals' first playoff game this year, against the Astros in the division series. He's had at least one hit in every game since, and entered the game as the Royals' top hitter in the playoffs with a .356 batting average.

The 14-game streak ties for the longest in a single postseason, matching Manny Ramirez of the Red Sox in 2004 and Marquis Grissom of the Braves in 1995.

The single also gave Escobar 22 postseason hits, which ties the Yankees' Derek Jeter as the most in a postseason by a shortstop.

Zobrist is seeing double. His sixth-inning two-base hit was his eighth of the playoffs, and that also matched a postseason record.

SHANE KEYSER

Zobrist's double was his fourth of the World Series, and it led to the Royals' second run. Lorenzo Cain followed with a single up the middle to cut the Mets' lead to 3-2.

- *Blair Kerkhoff*

JOHN SLEEZER

Ben Zobrist points to the heavens after hitting a double.

JOHN SLEEZER

Royals shortstop Alcides Escobar singled in the first inning and set a franchise record with a 14-game postseason hitting streak.

Infield defense costs New York

Before Game 3 of the 2015 World Series began, it was said that if Royals hitters could keep the ball on the ground, the Mets infielders might betray the Mets pitchers.

That happened in the eighth inning of the Royals' 5-3 victory in Game 4 Saturday.

With one down and runners on first and second base, Eric Hosmer hit a ground ball to Mets second baseman Daniel Murphy.

The ball got through Murphy and the runner on second base - Ben Zobrist - scored to tie the game. That opened the inning up, and after two more singles the Royals had a 5-3 lead. And because Wade Davis is the closer for the Royals, it was a lead they would not give back.

Routine plays

Saturday night Citi Field turned into a Halloween House of Horrors for the Royals. But there were some weird things happening.

- The Royals lost a base runner when Zobrist stepped across home plate while Alcides Escobar was busy stealing second. Zobrist interfered with catcher Travis d'Arnaud's throw and that turned into a double play; Zobrist struck out and Escobar was called out on batter's interference.

- After catching a fly ball, Alex Rios forgot the number of outs with a runner on third base. There's some doubt as to whether Rios could have thrown the runner out if had known the right number of outs, but it would have been nice to find out.

- It's uncertain if Danny Duffy could have beaten Curtis Granderson to the bag even with a good jump, but once again Eric Hosmer fielded a grounder, looked up and had no pitcher on first base to throw to.

The Royals will make it a lot easier on themselves if they make routine plays and pay attention to fundamentals.

- *Lee Judge*

SHANE KEYSER

Kansas City Royals right fielder Alex Rios dived to catch a fly ball hit by Mets second baseman Daniel Murphy in the first inning of Game 4.

SHANE KEYSER

After opening the sixth with a double, Ben Zobrist scored on Lorenzo Cain's single up the middle.

Story of the game

BY PETE GRATHOFF

1 Unusual double play

No brush-back pitch this time to Alcides Escobar, but he swung and missed at the first pitch. Facing a 1-2 count, he singled and extended his postseason hitting streak to 14 games, a Royals record. Ben Zobrist struck out, and his swing took him over the plate. Escobar was running at the time, and Travis d'Arnaud couldn't complete his throw. Interference was called, and Escobar was out. Chris Young set the Mets down in order in the bottom half.

0-0
KC-NYM

2 Chris Young is perfect

Salvador Perez had a two-out single against Mets starter Steven Matz, but he didn't budge. Alex Gordon followed with a grounder to first that ended the inning. Young struck out Yoenis Cespedes as part of another 1-2-3 inning.

0-0
KC-NYM

3 Rios' big mistake

Matz had his first perfect inning, and Michael Conforto quickly gave the Mets the lead. He hit a home run to right field. The ball traveled 395 feet, and fans at Citi Field were joyous. Wilmer Flores followed with a single. He took second on a wild pitch and moved to third on Matz's sacrifice. Curtis Granderson lifted a fly to right that Alex Rios caught. He jogged in a few steps, apparently losing track of the number of outs, and threw home late as Flores scored. The Royals challenged that Flores left early, but the replay officials didn't have conclusive evidence to overturn it.

2-0
NYM-KC

4 Pitchers rule the inning

This was Matz's best inning. He struck out Zobrist and Lorenzo Cain looking. Eric Hosmer then grounded to second. This was Young's best inning, too. He struck out Cespedes and Lucas Duda, then got d'Arnaud to pop out to Hosmer.

2-0
NYM-KC

5 Each team scores

With one out, Perez hit a ball to center that Cespedes appeared to think he could get to at first. It bounced in front of him and hit off his leg and scooted away. Perez ended up with a double. Gordon singled home Perez. After Rios flied out, pinch hitter Kendrys Morales singled and Gordon took second. However, Escobar flied out to right, ending the threat. Danny Duffy took the hill for the Royals,

and Conforto greeted him with a home run to right-center. Granderson singled with two outs but was caught stealing.

3-1
NYM-KC

6 Royals cut margin

Zobrist opened with a double and scored on Cain's single up the middle. Jon Niese entered, and Cain stole second before Hosmer flied to center. Mike Moustakas grounded to third, and Bartolo Colon took over. His pickoff throw to second went into center field, and Cain took third. However, Perez struck out, leaving Cain at third. Luke Hochevar tossed a clean inning.

3-2
NYM-KC

7 Quick work

Addison Reed tossed a 1-2-3 inning, though Gordon hit a ball deep to right and Rios lined to short. Pinch hitter Jarrod Dyson struck out. Ryan Madson also breezed through the inning, ending it with strikeouts of d'Arnaud and Conforto.

3-2
NYM-KC

8 Spooky eighth

Tyler Clippard started the inning and issued one-out walks to Zobrist and Cain, and the Mets turned to Jeurys Familia, and he induced a grounder to Daniel Murphy at second. The ball scooted under Murphy's glove and Zobrist sped home. Moustakas then singled to right and Cain scored as the Royals took the lead. Next it was Perez, whose single scored Cain. Just like that, it was a two-run Royals lead. Ned Yost brought in Wade Davis to start the Mets' half. Unsurprisingly, he set the Mets down in order.

5-3
KC-NYM

9 Just one win to go

The Royals went down in order in the top of the inning, but it mattered little. The Mets made some noise with consecutive one-out singles by Murphy and Cespedes, but Duda hit a soft liner to Moustakas, who doubled Cespedes off first.

5-3
KC-NYM

ROYALS 5, METS 3

Kansas City	AB	R	H	BI	BB	SO	Avg.
A.Escobar ss	5	0	1	0	0	0	.250
Zobrist 2b	3	2	1	0	1	2	.278
L.Cain cf	3	1	1	1	1	1	.176
Hosmer 1b	4	1	0	0	0	1	.133
Moustakas 3b	4	0	1	1	0	0	.353
S.Perez c	4	1	3	1	0	1	.412
A.Gordon lf	4	0	1	1	0	0	.286
Rios rf	3	0	0	0	0	0	.167
Orlando rf	1	0	0	0	0	1	.200
C.Young p	1	0	0	0	0	1	.000
a-K.Morales ph	1	0	1	0	0	0	.222
D.Duffy p	0	0	0	0	0	0	---
Hochevar p	0	0	0	0	0	0	---
b-J.Dyson ph	1	0	0	0	0	1	.000
Madson p	0	0	0	0	0	0	---
W.Davis p	1	0	0	0	0	1	.000
Totals	35	5	9	4	2	9	

New York	AB	R	H	BI	BB	SO	Avg.
Granderson rf	3	0	1	1	0	0	.250
D.Wright 3b	3	0	0	0	1	1	.211
Dan.Murphy 2b	4	0	1	0	0	0	.176
Cespedes cf-lf	4	0	1	0	0	2	.176
Duda 1b	4	0	0	0	0	1	.294
T.d'Arnaud c	3	0	0	0	0	1	.188
Conforto lf	3	2	2	2	0	1	.300
Clippard p	0	0	0	0	0	0	---
Familia p	0	0	0	0	0	0	---
Nieuwenhuis cf	0	0	0	0	0	0	.000
W.Flores ss	3	1	1	0	0	2	.077
Matz p	1	0	0	0	0	0	.000
Niese p	0	0	0	0	0	0	---
B.Colon p	0	0	0	0	0	0	---
A.Reed p	0	0	0	0	0	0	---
Lagares cf	0	0	0	0	0	0	.375
c-K.Johnson ph	1	0	0	0	0	0	.000
Robles p	0	0	0	0	0	0	---
Totals	29	3	6	3	1	8	

Kansas City	000	011	030	—	5	9	0
New York	002	010	000	—	3	6	2

a-singled for C.Young in the 5th. b-struck out for Hochevar in the 7th. c-flied out for Lagares in the 8th.

E: B.Colon (1), Dan.Murphy (1). **LOB:** Kansas City 5, New York 2. **2B:** Zobrist (4), S.Perez (2). **HR:** Conforto (1), off C.Young; Conforto (2), off D.Duffy. **RBIs:** L.Cain (1), Moustakas (3), S.Perez (1), A.Gordon (3), Granderson (4), Conforto 2 (4). **SB:** L.Cain (2). **CS:** Granderson (1). **S:** Matz. **SF:** Granderson.

Runners left in scoring position: Kansas City 3 (A.Escobar, S.Perez, A.Gordon); New York 1 (Duda). **RISP:** Kansas City 4 for 10; New York 0 for 1. **GIDP:** A.Gordon. **DP:** Kansas City 1 (Moustakas, Hosmer); New York 2 (T.d'Arnaud, T.d'Arnaud), (Dan.Murphy, Duda).

Kansas City	IP	H	R	ER	BB	SO	NP	ERA
C.Young	4	2	2	2	1	3	58	2.57
D.Duffy	1	2	1	1	0	1	18	3.86
Hochevar	1	0	0	0	0	1	11	0.00
Madson W, 1-0	1	0	0	0	0	2	16	0.00
W.Davis S, 1	2	2	0	0	0	2	27	0.00

New York	IP	H	R	ER	BB	SO	NP	ERA
Matz	5	7	2	2	0	5	84	3.60
Niese	⅔	0	0	0	0	0	11	7.36
B.Colon	⅓	0	0	0	0	1	10	0.00
A.Reed	1	0	0	0	0	1	20	0.00
Clippard L, 0-1	⅓	0	2	2	2	0	17	9.00
Familia	⅔	2	1	0	0	0	9	3.00
Robles	1	0	0	0	0	2	15	0.00

Matz pitched to 2 batters in the 6th.

Blown saves: Familia (2). **Holds:** Clippard (2), B.Colon (1), Niese (1), A.Reed (1). **Inherited runners-scored:** Niese 1-0, B.Colon 1-0, Familia 2-2. **WP:** C.Young.

Umpires: Home, Jim Wolf; First, Alfonso Marquez; Second, Gary Cederstrom; Third, Mike Everitt; Left, Mark Carlson; Right, Mike Winters. **Time:** 3:29. **Att:** 44,815.

The Mets' Michael Conforto rounded the bases after hitting a solo home run off Royals starting pitcher Chris Young in the third inning. It was a small hiccup in an otherwise stellar performance. Young allowed just two hits in four innings of work.

Two innings is fine with closer Davis

NEW YORK

One inning or two. This time of year, it makes no difference to Royals closer Wade Davis.

The Royals worked their closer in the eighth and ninth innings to protect a 5-3 lead Saturday and give them a 3-1 edge in the World Series. The Royals can close it out in Game 5 on Sunday.

After the Royals scored three in the top of the eighth, there was no doubt manager Ned Yost would extend Davis.

"It's the World Series," Davis said. "You have a lot more adrenaline to wind up and go out there and give everything you've got. A couple more outs really doesn't change anything."

Rest was the key. Davis hadn't pitched in the series since Game 1 last Tuesday.

"He was the most rested guy we had down there today," Yost said. "We knew if we had the lead in the eighth inning, unless it was a three-, four-, five-run lead, we were going to go to Wade in that inning."

Davis has been even more machine-like in the postseason than the regular season, when he took over the closer's role from Greg Holland in August and wound up with 17 saves, surrendering a miniscule seven earned runs in 67⅓ innings for a 0.94 ERA.

In the playoffs, Davis has now appeared in seven games, throwing 9⅔ innings without surrendering a run.

Saturday, Davis breezed through the eighth, but had to work out of trouble in the ninth after Daniel Murphy and Yoenis Cesepedes singled with one out.

Lucas Duda then hit a soft liner to third baseman Mike Moustakas. Instead of freezing to see if the ball would be hit through the infield, Cesepedes took a couple of steps toward second, and Moustakas threw him to first and completed a double play.

- Blair Kerkhoff

JILL TOYOSHIBA

Kansas City Royals left fielder Alex Gordon broke his bat on a grounder for an out in the second inning.

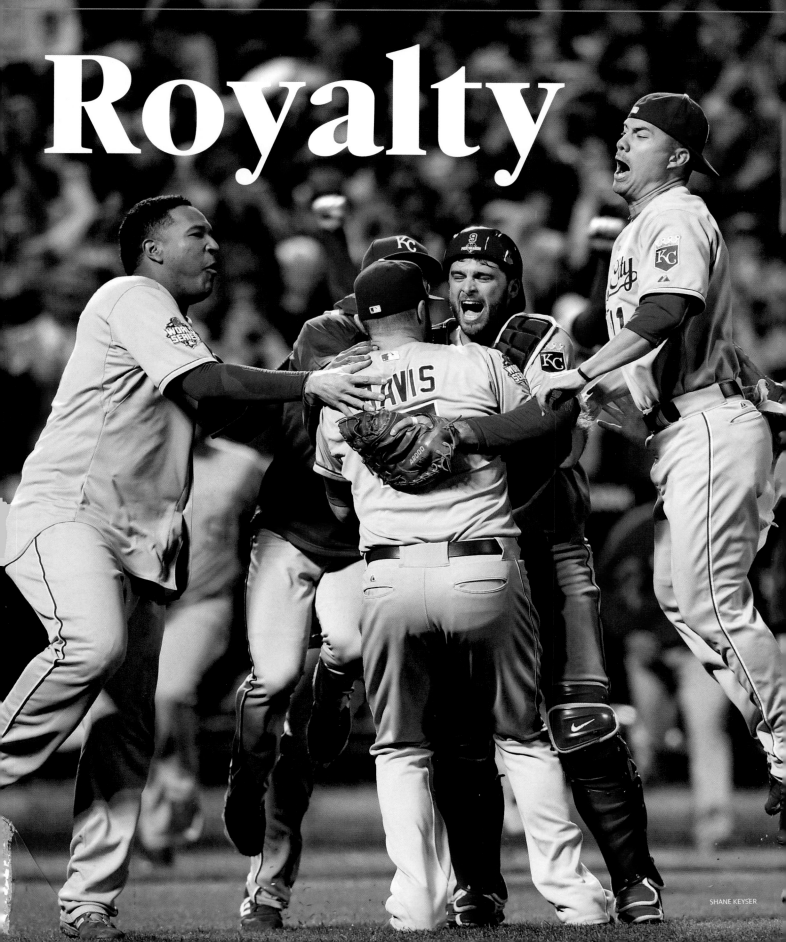

Royalty

SHANE KEYSER

WORLD SERIES GAME 5

	1 2 3	4 5 6	7 8 9	10 11 12		R	H	E
Kansas City	000	000	002	005	—	7	10	1
New York	100	001	000	000	—	2	4	2

THE KANSAS CITY STAR

11/2/15

An extra-special win

The Royals are the World Series champs after beating the Mets 7-2 in 12 innings

KC ties it with two runs in the ninth inning of Game 5

Christian Colon's RBI single in 12th gives them the lead

_____

BY ANDY McCULLOUGH

NEW YORK

The best Royals team in a generation assembled for one last time at 12:34 a.m. local time, converging in the center of Citi Field, the last mountain this group ascended. With a 7-2 victory in 12 innings over the Mets, the Royals captured the 111th World Series in five games, collected their first title since 1985 and provided a lifetime of memories for fans who stuck with this franchise through 29 years without a playoff appearance.

This group, assembled by general manager Dayton Moore and shepherded through the season by manager Ned Yost, stands atop Major League Baseball. When Moore took over the baseball operations of this franchise, the team resided in baseball's basement, a running joke among its peers. Now they stood alone. So when the final 95-mph fastball of Wade Davis reached the glove of catcher Drew Butera, the rest of the team bounded over the dugout steps to celebrate the accomplishment.

Charging in from the dugout were Christian Colon, the man who drove in the winning run, and Jarrod Dyson, the man who scored it. Both were mothballed on the Kansas City bench for most of the playoffs. Both emerged in the 12th inning to complete the run of a lifetime.

Dyson hopped out of the dugout to replace Salvador Perez at

DAVID EULITT

The Royals' Christian Colon (center) was congratulated by Salvador Perez (left) and Kendrys Morales after Colon drove in the go-ahead run and later scored during their five-run 12th inning.

first base after Perez led off with a single against Mets reliever Addison Reed. Dyson proceeded to utilize his finest skill, the speed that convinced the Royals to stick with him as a 50th-round draft pick in 2006. So he stole second base.

Two batters later, Colon picked up a bat for the first time this postseason. Reed refused to throw him a fastball. Colon waited until a fifth slider crossed the plate. Then he punched the go-ahead single into left field and thumped his chest at first. In the aftermath, the Mets bullpen imploded. The Royals notched four more runs, the last three on a bases-clearing double by Lorenzo Cain.

But linger, for a moment, on Colon at first base. His teammates clambered over their dugout to salute him. He now had a career highlight to pair with his game-tying infield single from the American League Wild Card game in 2014.

That night, so many months ago, solidified the ethos of this team. Pushed to the brink, the Royals do not break. Instead, it is their opponents who buckle.

On Sunday, in the final flourish of the season, the team followed its formula. It strung together a ninth-inning comeback with timely hitting and daring displays on the bases.

As the bottom of the eighth inning wound down, the fans at Citi Field shouted for another inning from Matt Harvey. He had blanked the Royals for the duration of the evening. He had struck out nine. Inside his own dugout, he argued with manager Terry Collins, insisting on staying in the game.

Harvey wanted the ninth. He wanted the Royals. Perhaps history will forgive him for his impudence, because the Royals did not.

The rally started in the most unlikely of ways for Kansas City. Down two strikes, Lorenzo Cain battled his way back for a walk. The crowd stirred. Harvey tried to drive a 94-mph fastball past Eric Hosmer's knees. Hosmer did not let the baseball pass, thumping an opposite-field, RBI double.

"We always feel like we're in it," Hosmer said. "We never feel like we're out of any game."

The hit halved the score and petrified the park. Collins fetched Harvey and handed the baseball over to Jeurys

Familia. Before this series, the presence of Familia almost guaranteed a Mets victory. Yet in the first four games here, he had already blown two saves. A third would soon follow.

Guile ruled the day. After Mike Moustakas advanced Hosmer to third base, Perez stepped to the plate. He tapped a grounder toward third baseman David Wright. As Wright whirled to throw to first, Hosmer broke for the plate. A precise throw from Lucas Duda would have ended the game.

Duda did not make a precise throw. His volley home sprayed wide. Hosmer slid head-first across the plate to tie the game. The Royals' dugout jumped with joy.

When their season ended last October, with the tying run stranded at third base in Game 7 of the World Series, the Royals felt the sort of heartbreak that lingers through the winter. The players mourned the loss and sought to convert the pain into fuel for 2015.

At 3 p.m. on Oct. 12, Kansas City trailed Houston by four runs. Six outs remained in their season. Then Alex Rios hit the first pitch he saw from reliever Will Harris into left field. Escobar fished for a curve and found a hit. Ben Zobrist cracked a line drive into center field, where outfielder Carlos Gomez declined to dive.

The seventh comeback of the postseason occurred on Saturday night. The victory allowed the Royals to hit their pillows dreaming of a title.

The players tried to treat this like any other ordinary day.

As the players warmed up, Edinson Volquez prepared inside his clubhouse. He had only rejoined the team night before. He learned minutes after leaving the mound in Game 1 about the death of his father. Volquez retreated to the Dominican Republic for the memorial service.

While Volquez was away, the team maintained minimal contact with him. Pitching coach Dave Eiland felt uncomfortable asking Volquez about baseball when his loss was so fresh. Volquez assured Eiland he could pitch.

On the third pitch of the game, Volquez allowed a change-up to flatten across the heart of the plate. Curtis Granderson boomed a solo shot over the center-field fence.

JOHN SLEEZER

Royals starter Edinson Volquez showed his mettle again in Game 5 of the World Series, pitching six quality innings and striking out five just days after returning home to his native Dominican Republic to bury his father.

JOHN SLEEZER

Royals manager Ned Yost watched from the dugout in the sixth inning while Christian Colon waited in the background.

Royals center fielder Lorenzo Cain pointed back to first baseman Eric Hosmer after Cain scored on a double hit by Hosmer in the ninth inning.

Eric Hosmer reacted after scoring in the ninth inning.

Volquez recovered to avoid further damage in the inning, but a one-run lead against Harvey looked daunting.

A two-run lead looked even worse. Volquez yielded his second run in the sixth inning when Duda lofted a sacrifice fly.

During Game 1, Harvey generated only two strikeouts. He matched that number in Sunday's first inning.

Harvey does not deal in deception. He piles power upon power. His fastball approaches triple digits. His slider clocks at 90 mph. His change-up resides only a few ticks lower.

In the fourth, Harvey displayed the depth and breadth of his arsenal. With the count at 3-1, Cain chased a high fastball. Harvey finished him off with a change-up, down and in. Hosmer flailed at a curveball for a second strikeout.

The last victim was Moustakas. Harvey flipped a pair of curveballs for strikes. Then he blazed a 98-mph fastball past Moustakas to strike out the side. Harvey pumped his fist as he headed for his dugout.

The celebration looked premature. The Royals, after all, do their most devastating damage in the later innings. Harvey would receive a reminder in the ninth.

Harvey refused to bend. When Alex Gordon walked in the fifth, Harvey struck out the next two batters. When Zobrist rifled a single in the sixth, Harvey fanned Cain and induced a ground-ball out from Hosmer. When Moustakas led off the seventh with a hit, Harvey stranded him at first.

As Harvey toiled in the eighth, Familia warmed up in the bullpen. But inserting him into the game looked dicey. The night would belong to Harvey.

So he headed back out for the ninth shouldering the responsibility. After Hosmer's hit, Harvey handed the baseball to his manager and watched his closer stumble for the third time in five games.

The ending would not come until three innings later. But Citi Field loomed as the last mountain for the Royals to climb. As the ballpark emptied, this team stood alone.

"I forgot about last year already," Perez said. "In 2015, we are No. 1."

Royals make comeback victories routine

The Royals have come back and won eight of their postseason games.

AMERICAN LEAGUE DIVISION SERIES

- **The Game:** Game 2 in Kansas City. **The Deficit:** Royals trailed 4-1 in the third. **How they came back:** The Royals manufactured a run in the bottom of the third, and Eric Hosmer sparked a two-run outburst in the sixth with a bloop single to left. Ben Zobrist capped the comeback with an RBI single in the seventh in a 5-4 victory.

- **The Game:** Game 4 in Houston. **The Deficit:** Royals trailed 6-2 in the eighth. **How they came back:** Facing elimination, the Royals opened the eighth with five straight singles and tied the game on an error by Astros shortstop Carlos Correa. Alex Gordon broke a 6-6 deadlock with an RBI ground-out, and Wade Davis came on for a two-inning save in a 9-6 victory.

- **The Game:** Game 5 in Kansas City. **The Deficit:** Royals trailed 2-0 in the fourth. **How they came back:** Starter Johnny Cueto surrendered two early runs, but the offense picked him up, answering with a run in the fourth and three more in the fifth. Alex Rios came up with the key hit, stroking a two-run double that turned a 2-1 deficit into a 3-2 lead. The Royals advanced to the ALCS with a 7-2 win.

AMERICAN LEAGUE CHAMPIONSHIP SERIES

- **The Game:** Game 2 in Kansas City. **The Deficit:** Royals trailed 3-0 in the seventh. **How they came back:** When Ben Zobrist's shallow pop-up fell to the turf in right field, the Royals exploded for five runs against Toronto ace David Price. Gordon's double to right-center scored Mike Moustakas and broke a 3-3 tie in an eventual 6-3 victory.

WORLD SERIES

- **The Game:** Game 1 in Kansas City. **The Deficit:** Royals trailed 4-3 in the ninth. **How they came back:** Gordon stepped to the plate against Mets closer Jeurys Familia with one out and nobody on. Gordon crushed a solo homer to center field. Five innings later, in the bottom of the 14th, the Royals completed the 5-4 victory.

- **The Game:** Game 2 in Kansas City. **The Deficit:** Royals trailed 1-0 in the fifth. **How they came back:** The Royals broke out against Mets starter Jacob deGrom in the bottom of the fifth, scoring four runs as Cueto went the distance in a 7-1 victory.

- **The Game:** Game 4 in New York. **The Deficit:** Royals trailed 3-1 in the sixth. **How they came back:** After cutting the Mets' lead to 3-2 in the sixth, the Royals struck for three runs in the eighth, taking advantage of an error by second baseman Daniel Murphy in a 5-3 win.

- **The Game:** Game 5 in New York. **The Deficit:** Royals trailed 2-0 in the ninth. **How they came back:** Hosmer doubled home Lorenzo Cain and scored the tying run in the ninth on a ground-out when first baseman Lucas Duda threw wide to the plate. The Royals scored the go-ahead run in the 12th on Christian Colon's single and ended up winning 7-2.

SHANE KEYSER

Mets second baseman Daniel Murphy slid into second while Royals second baseman Ben Zobrist turned a double play to end the fourth inning.

JOHN SLEEZER

Royals relief pitcher Wade Davis (left) and first baseman Eric Hosmer celebrated after finishing off the Mets.

Story of the game

BY PETE GRATHOFF

1 **Mets score first**
Alcides Escobar struck out starting the game, and Ben Zobrist flied to center. Lorenzo Cain singled, reaching base for the 20th straight playoff game. He stole second, but Eric Hosmer struck out. Curtis Granderson homered to right-center field and gave the Mets an early lead.

1-0
NYM-KC

2 **Royals don't take advantage**
Mike Moustakas' grounder to third was booted by David Wright. However, Salvador Perez, Alex Gordon and Alex Rios grounded to short. Lucas Duda walked for the Mets, but Travis d'Arnaud hit into a double play. Michael Conforto then struck out.

1-0
NYM-KC

3 **Edinson Volquez, hit machine**
Edinson Volquez opened the inning with a single, but he was erased on a 4-6-3 double play off the bat of Escobar. Zobrist flied to right, ending the inning. Volquez had an easy inning, setting the Mets down in order, capped by a strikeout of Granderson.

1-0
NYM-KC

4 **No contact for Royals**
Harvey mowed through the Royals, striking out Cain, Hosmer and Moustakas. Wright struck out for the Mets, but Daniel Murphy drew a walk. However, Yoenis Cespedes grounded into a 5-4-3 double play.

1-0
NYM-KC

5 **Three more Harvey strikeouts**
Matt Harvey got three strikeouts again, although Gordon drew a one-out walk. Duda walked leading off. But d'Arnaud flied to to left, and Conforto grounded to first. Duda took second, and Flores was walked intentionally. Harvey grounded out.

1-0
NYM-KC

6 **Mets double lead**
Zobrist singled with one out, but Harvey struck out Cain, and Hosmer grounded out. Granderson walked leading off and Wright singled. Murphy's ground ball was booted by Hosmer. Cespedes fouled a ball off his knee and collapsed in pain. He stayed in the game and popped out to Escobar. Duda's sacrifice fly scored Granderson, but Volquez got d'Arnaud to ground out to Moustakas.

2-0
NYM-KC

7 **Herrera enters**
Moustakas opened with a single, but Perez popped to third base. Gordon flied out and Rios grounded to third. Kelvin Herrera came in and gave up a single to Conforto. But Flores hit into a 6-4-3 double play and then Harvey grounded out.

2-0
NYM-KC

8 **Silent bats**
Harvey seemed to be in control. Paulo Orlando, who was in right field, flied to right. Escobar popped out to short, and Zobrist flied to center. The Mets couldn't do anything against Herrera as he struck out the side.

2-0
NYM-KC

9 **They did it again**
Harvey talked Mets manager Terry Collins into staying in the game. It was a mistake. Cain drew a walk and stole second. Hosmer doubled to left and Cain scored. That was it for Harvey as Jeurys Familia relieved. Moustakas grounded to first and Hosmer took third. Perez grounded softly toward short, and Wright cut off the ball. He looked at Hosmer, then threw to first for the out. With no one near third base, Hosmer held his ground and then broke for home and scored easily. Duda threw wild from first base, but Hosmer likely would have been safe anyway. Herrera set the Mets down in order.

2-2
KC-NYM

12 **Your World Series champions**
Perez dunked a single to right. Jarrod Dyson pinch ran and stole second. Gordon grounded to first, and pinch hitter Christian Colon singled home Dyson. Escobar had a RBI double and Cain hit a bases-clearing double. Wade Davis did his thing, and it was over.

7-2
KC-NYM

ROYALS 7, METS 2, 12 INN.

Kansas City	AB	R	H	BI	BB	SO	Avg.
A.Escobar ss	6	1	1	1	0	2	.231
Zobrist 2b	5	1	1	0	1	0	.261
L.Cain cf	5	1	2	3	1	2	.227
Hosmer 1b	6	1	2	1	0	2	.190
Moustakas 3b	6	0	1	0	0	1	.304
S.Perez c	5	0	1	1	0	1	.364
1-J.Dyson pr	0	1	0	0	0	0	.000
Butera c	0	0	0	0	0	0	---
A.Gordon lf	4	0	0	0	1	0	.222
Rios rf	3	0	0	0	0	1	.133
K.Herrera p	0	0	0	0	0	0	---
a-K.Morales ph	1	0	0	0	0	1	.200
Hochevar p	0	0	0	0	0	0	---
c-C.Colon ph	1	1	1	1	0	0	1.000
W.Davis p	0	0	0	0	0	0	.000
Volquez p	2	0	1	0	0	1	.500
Orlando rf	3	1	0	0	0	0	.125
Totals	47	7	10	7	3	11	

New York	AB	R	H	BI	BB	SO	Avg.
Granderson rf	4	2	1	1	1	2	.250
D.Wright 3b	5	0	1	0	0	3	.208
Dan.Murphy 2b	3	0	0	0	2	2	.150
Cespedes cf	3	0	0	0	0	0	.150
Lagares cf	2	0	0	0	0	0	.300
Duda 1b	2	0	0	1	2	1	.263
T.d'Arnaud c	5	0	0	0	0	1	.143
Conforto lf	5	0	2	0	0	0	.333
W.Flores ss	4	0	0	0	1	1	.059
Harvey p	3	0	0	0	0	0	.000
Familia p	0	0	0	0	0	0	---
b-K.Johnson ph	1	0	0	0	0	0	.000
Niese p	0	0	0	0	0	0	---
A.Reed p	0	0	0	0	0	0	---
B.Colon p	0	0	0	0	0	0	---
Totals	37	2	4	2	6	11	

Kansas City	000	000	002	005	—	7	10	1
New York	100	001	000	000	—	2	4	2

a-struck out for K.Herrera in the 10th.
b-fouled out for Familia in the 10th. c-singled for Hochevar in the 12th.
  1-ran for S.Perez in the 12th.
  E: Hosmer (2), D.Wright (2), Dan.Murphy (2). **LOB:** Kansas City 7, New York 6. **2B:** A.Escobar (1), L.Cain (1), Hosmer (1). **HR:** Granderson (3), off Volquez. **RBIs:** A.Escobar (4), L.Cain 3 (4), Hosmer (6), S.Perez (2), C.Colon (1), Granderson (5), Duda (2). **SB:** L.Cain 2 (4), Hosmer (1), J.Dyson (1). **SF:** Duda.
  Runners left in scoring position: Kansas City 3 (Hosmer, Moustakas 2); New York 3 (Harvey, T.d'Arnaud, W.Flores).
RISP: Kansas City 4 for 11; New York 0 for 5. **Runners moved up:** Hosmer, Moustakas, S.Perez, A.Gordon, Conforto. **GIDP:** A.Escobar, Cespedes, T.d'Arnaud, W.Flores. **DP:** Kansas City 3 (Zobrist, Hosmer), (Moustakas, Zobrist, Hosmer), (A.Escobar, Zobrist, Hosmer); New York 1 (Dan.Murphy, W.Flores, Duda).

Kansas City	IP	H	R	ER	BB	SO	NP	ERA
Volquez	6	2	2	1	5	5	90	3.00
K.Herrera	3	1	0	0	0	3	33	0.00
Hochevar W, 1-0	2	0	0	0	1	0	26	0.00
W.Davis	1	1	0	0	0	3	20	0.00

New York	IP	H	R	ER	BB	SO	NP	ERA
Harvey	8	5	2	2	2	9	111	3.21
Familia	2	0	0	0	0	2	24	1.80
Niese	1	1	0	0	0	0	13	5.79
A.Reed L, 0-1	1/3	3	5	4	1	0	28	9.82
B.Colon	2/3	1	0	0	0	0	10	0.00

Harvey pitched to 2 batters in the 9th.
  Blown save: Familia (3). **Inherited runners-scored:** Familia 1-1, B.Colon 3-3. **IBB:** off Volquez (W.Flores), off A.Reed (Zobrist).

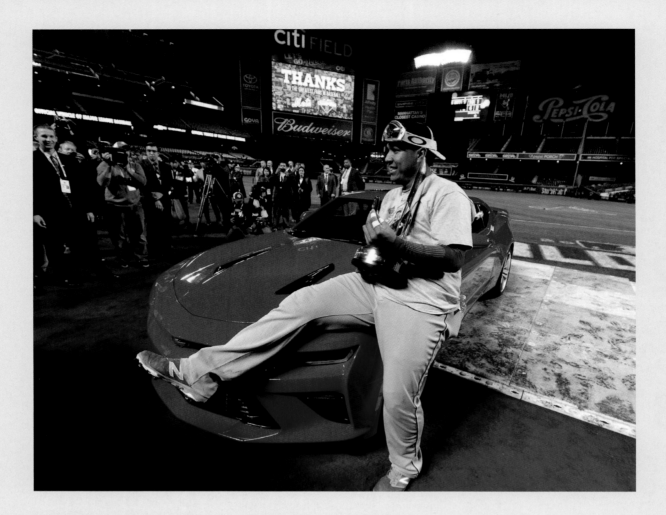

Salvador Perez, World Series MVP

His single in the 12th inning started five-run rally

A year ago, Royals catcher Salvador Perez made the final out of the World Series with the tying run just 90 feet from home.

On Sunday night, he opened the 12th inning of Game 5 with a single down the right-field line. That opened the door to a five-run inning, and the Royals won 7-2 and were crowned World Series champions.

Perez was chosen World Series MVP.

"I forgot about last year already," Perez said. "In 2015, we are No. 1."

Perez batted .364 (8 for 22) in the World Series. In addition to his single that started the 12th-inning rally, Perez's ground-out in the ninth inning allowed Eric Hosmer to scamper home with the tying run.

"We never quit," Perez said. "Never put our head down. Never think about, 'OK game is over.'"

It was a rough series for Perez. He seemed to get hit by a foul ball off one of his body parts every single game.

"Now I don't feel pain. I don't feel nothing," he said.

In the American League Division Series against Houston, Perez took a foul tip off the mask in Game 4 that left him temporarily dazed. He also was hit by a pitch. And Perez was in a minor car accident while in Houston.

"He's never going to say nothing," Royals manager Ned Yost told reporters. "He's as tough as they come. You just know that even if you ask him, he's going to tell you he's fine, so no sense of asking him."

- Pete Grathoff

The Associated Press contributed to this story.

Confetti shot over the crowd as Royals fans celebrated the team's World Series victory in the Power & Light District.

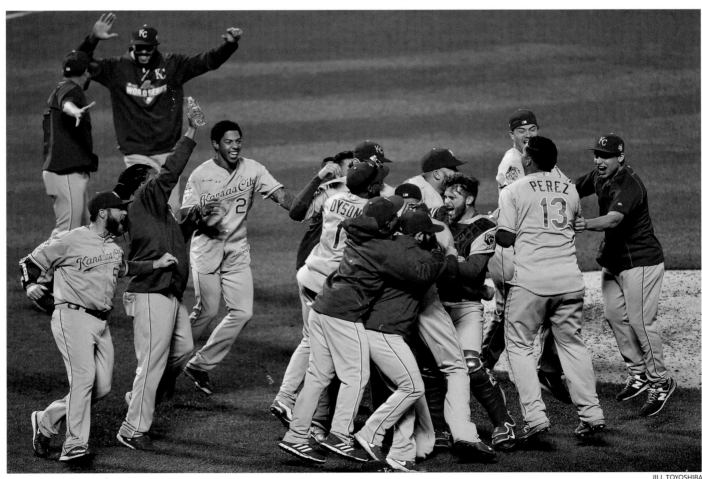

The Royals celebrated moments after defeating the Mets 7-2 to win the World Series at Citi Field in New York. Kansas City rallied to win its first title in 30 years.

The celebration that started in New York ignited a party in Kansas City that raged well into the night.

A city united

November 3, 2015

The Royals and hundreds of thousands of their fans came together to thank each other for a monumental season to remember.

ALLISON LONG

KEITH MYERS

ALLISON LONG

SHANE KEYSER

KEITH MYERS

KEITH MYERS

Kansas City takes the crown, on the playing field and off it, too

One of the famous phrases attributed to Satchel Paige, the great Kansas City baseball player, was this: "Don't look back. Something might be gaining on you."

This bit of wisdom applies to the Royals in two ways. In the 2015 postseason the Royals gained on and then overcame every opponent they faced.

And coming home with the World Series trophy means the Royals — and their fans — don't have to look back with longing and regret at 2014 or 1985 or all the fallow years in between.

When the Royals — once again in astounding fashion — came back and defeated the New York Mets Sunday night, 7-2 in 12 innings, they won the 2015 World Series four games to one.

But the team did much, much more than that during this endlessly exciting season.

Throughout the spring, summer and fall, the Royals helped bring this community together.

Fans from both sides of the state line, from Kansas City and all its suburbs, packed Kauffman Stadium.

Kansas City area residents wore the color blue not just at the ballpark but at shopping centers, supermarkets, on the Country Club Plaza, all around the town.

In the world of sports, the Royals became known for their aggressive hitting style in 2015. They slugged fastballs better than most other teams. And they were relentless, pulling out many comebacks during the year but, most notably, in the postseason, where they set a record for most runs scored (51) in the seventh inning or later.

This community has had that same kind of come-from-behind attitude in recent years, which explains a lot about the revival of Kansas City.

It took an aggressive effort to get projects off the ground after so many lackluster years of neglect in the urban core.

It took relentless leadership by political officials — as well as by voters who embraced opportunities to create a better city.

The naysayers who said a decade ago that it wasn't a good idea to build Sprint Center downtown? Wrong. The highly successful arena on Grand Boulevard will mark the starting point of the World Series victory parade on Tuesday, and the route will feature an up-and-coming downtown.

The doubters who predicted the Power & Light District would be a wasteland of inactivity? Also wrong. Fans packed the entertainment space shoulder-to-shoulder Sunday night and partied on long after the Royals became world champions.

The negative nannies on the streetcar and nearby redevelopment? So far, off base. The city, coincidentally, took possession of the first vehicle on Monday.

Much like the Royals — who wandered in baseball's netherworld for so many years, losing more than 100 games four times in five years starting in 2002 — Kansas City has staged a comeback of its own.

There's more: This Royals team is so good and so young, and has been to two straight World Series, we could see Kansas City back on baseball's biggest postseason stage for years to come.

But for now, in early November, for the first time in 30 years, this metropolitan area will bask in the attention that comes with a World Series crown.

And we will wear it proudly.

— Editorial, The Kansas City Star, Nov. 1, 2015

Season Stats

Kansas City Royals Postseason - Batting

NAME	GP	AB	R	H	2B	3B	HR	RBI	TB	BB	SO	SB	BA	OBP	SLG	OPS
Christian Colon	1	1	1	1	0	0	0	1	1	0	0	0	1.000	1.000	1.000	2.000
Edinson Volquez	5	2	0	1	0	0	0	0	1	0	1	0	.500	.500	.500	1.000
Alcides Escobar	16	70	13	23	4	3	1	9	36	0	10	1	.329	.347	.514	.861
Ben Zobrist	16	66	15	20	8	0	2	6	34	7	6	1	.303	.365	.515	.880
Paulo Orlando	12	11	3	3	0	0	0	1	3	0	2	0	.273	.250	.273	.523
Alex Rios	16	48	6	13	2	0	1	6	18	3	10	1	.271	.314	.375	.689
Salvador Perez	16	58	10	15	3	0	4	8	30	4	9	0	.259	.328	.517	.845
Lorenzo Cain	16	62	11	16	2	0	1	11	21	11	14	6	.258	.365	.339	.704
Kendrys Morales	16	51	5	13	0	0	4	10	25	4	12	0	.255	.304	.490	.794
Alex Gordon	16	54	10	13	4	0	2	6	23	8	14	0	.241	.349	.426	.775
Mike Moustakas	16	65	5	14	1	0	1	8	18	3	8	0	.215	.257	.277	.534
Eric Hosmer	16	66	10	14	2	0	1	17	19	3	17	1	.212	.236	.288	.524
Jarrod Dyson	6	4	1	0	0	0	0	0	0	0	2	3	.000	.000	.000	.000
Chris Young	4	1	0	0	0	0	0	0	0	0	1	0	.000	.000	.000	.000
Wade Davis	8	1	0	0	0	0	0	0	0	0	1	0	.000	.000	.000	.000
Drew Butera	3	1	0	0	0	0	0	0	0	1	0	0	.000	.500	.000	.500
Raul Mondesi	1	1	0	0	0	0	0	0	0	0	1	0	.000	.000	.000	.000
Ryan Madson	9	0	0	0	0	0	0	0	0	0	0	0	.000	.000	.000	.000
Luke Hochevar	9	0	0	0	0	0	0	0	0	0	0	0	.000	.000	.000	.000
Franklin Morales	3	0	0	0	0	0	0	0	0	0	0	0	.000	.000	.000	.000
Johnny Cueto	4	0	0	0	0	0	0	0	0	0	0	0	.000	.000	.000	.000
Kris Medlen	2	0	0	0	0	0	0	0	0	0	0	0	.000	.000	.000	.000
Danny Duffy	6	0	0	0	0	0	0	0	0	0	0	0	.000	.000	.000	.000
Yordano Ventura	5	0	0	0	0	0	0	0	0	0	0	0	.000	.000	.000	.000
Kelvin Herrera	11	0	0	0	0	0	0	0	0	0	0	0	.000	.000	.000	.000
Terrance Gore	2	0	0	0	0	0	0	0	0	0	0	1	.000	.000	.000	.000
Totals	16	562	90	146	26	3	17	83	229	44	108	14	.260	.316	.407	.724
Opponents	16	542	66	119	18	0	21	65	200	54	160	7	.220	.294	.369	.663

Kansas City Royals Postseason - Pitching

NAME	GP	GS	QS	W	L	SV	HLD	IP	H	ER	HR	BB	SO	K/9	P/GS	WHIP	ERA
Luke Hochevar	9	0	0	2	0	0	0	10.2	6	0	0	1	4	3.38	0.0	0.66	0.00
Wade Davis	8	0	0	1	0	4	0	10.2	6	0	0	3	18	15.19	0.0	0.84	0.00
Kelvin Herrera	11	0	0	1	0	0	3	13.2	10	1	0	3	22	14.49	0.0	0.95	0.66
Chris Young	4	2	0	1	0	0	0	15.2	8	5	2	6	18	10.34	68.0	0.89	2.87
Kris Medlen	2	0	0	0	0	0	0	6.0	3	2	2	1	8	12.00	0.0	0.67	3.00
Edinson Volquez	5	5	3	1	2	0	0	28.2	18	12	3	18	23	7.22	90.8	1.26	3.77
Johnny Cueto	4	4	2	2	1	0	0	25.0	17	15	3	10	19	6.84	96.3	1.08	5.40
Ryan Madson	9	0	0	2	0	0	2	8.1	12	5	4	3	15	16.20	0.0	1.80	5.40
Danny Duffy	6	0	0	1	0	0	0	6.0	7	4	2	0	9	13.50	0.0	1.17	6.00
Yordano Ventura	5	5	0	0	2	0	0	21.0	27	15	5	8	22	9.43	72.6	1.67	6.43
Franklin Morales	3	0	0	0	0	0	0	2.1	5	5	0	1	2	7.71	0.0	2.57	19.29
Totals	16	16	5	11	5	4	5	148.0	119	64	21	54	160	9.73	83.6	1.17	3.89